Finish

the

Race

Finish

the

Race

JON WALLER

Kravitz and Sons LLC
204 E Arlington Blvd. Suite B
Greenville, NC 27858

Published by Kravitz and Sons LLC.

ISBN: 979-8-89639-488-4 (sc)
ISBN: 979-8-89639-487-7 (e)
ISBN: 979-8-89639-489-1 (hb)

Library of Congress Control Number: 2026905748

Table of Contents

CHAPTER 1 — THE ITCH TO RACE

It is hard to pinpoint the instant that Jack Stone first began his attachment to racing triathlons. It probably was watching the Wide World of Sports coverage of the Ironman race in Kona, Hawaii and seeing two separate races typifying the "thrill of victory and the agony of defeat." Over several years, ABC presented in the gap between Football and Baseball seasons a show called the Wide World of Sports featuring sporting events all over the world, One of these was the little known sport of Triathlons. Months after the events, ABC would present highlights of the race, edited to create the atmosphere of the entire event, often showing what ABC termed the "Thrill of Victory and the Agony of Defeat." In advertising for the show ABC loved to show ski jumpers crashing from the ski jumps or race cars in fiery crashes. For the triathlons their show highlighted both the professional triathletes and the ordinary athletes that tested their limits just to finish. Their favorite event was the Ironman Championship in Kona Hawaii. It was difficult to cover a race that covered a 2.4 mile swim in the Pacific Ocean, 112 miles on bicycles along a rough highway around volcano fields and then a 26.2 footrace over some of those same roads to a finish near the start of the swim. Somehow through the miracle of editing, ABC seemed to do it well. There were no shortage of thrilling victories and agonizing defeats. Once ABC had filmed the race, they would go back and film interviews of the participants, both professional and amateur and work the interview clips into the presentation of the show. One such racer was a professional female triathlete that led the race at the 111-mile point and collapsed. The show revealed how she had triumphantly emerged from the waters of the bay, lead on the bike over the difficult and hot bike ride and then when she was nearly in sight of the finish, just faltered. She was not allowed to be aided by spectators other than their cheering support. But driven by the will to finish, she rose and then fell. She struggled to get up repeatedly until she finally crawled over the finish line while the top three female athletes who had trailed her passed her during her heroic struggles. This episode typified the ABC shows' "agony of defeat." Jack, when he saw the show, did not dwell on her defeat or her "failure to win." He would view this show many times over the years well before the creation of UTube. What had grabbed his attention was the struggle to finish that seized his attention. She had not lost, in his mind. She had finished. Finishing was what she had struggled to do and that is exactly what she had done. That struggle was the key to his interest.

But the race that was indelibly etched in his brain was the time that the ABC show featured a Massachusetts father and his disabled son racing at Kona. They were so inspiring and it was a pair that he knew well. He had raced against them while he lived in Dallas and later in the Falmouth Run in Massachusetts. They were a celebrity pair known throughout the running circuit. They raced as a tandem with the father pushing the son in a three wheeled buggy that is today called a stroller. For the race in Kona, the father would swim and pull his son on a floating raft for 2.4 miles in the ocean. Finishing the swim, he would carry his son up the steps to transition, position him on the front of a bicycle over the front wheel, suit himself up and then pedal over the bike course for 112 miles, balancing the young man on his handle bars and making sure both he and his son had the fluids they needed to complete the bike portion of the race. If he finished the bike leg of the race in the prescribed time, he would place his son in the jog stroller and push his son along 26.2 miles on the run. Fans watching the show rooted for them to finish each portion of the race. Thinking of it later, Jack seemed to recall that the bike was not even designed for speed. It probably had no more than three speeds. But the father was a strong dude. They failed in the attempt to finish but they had given it their all. Later in the broadcast, the program broke away for an intimate interview with the son given before the race. In it they asked the young man, who was a big fan of the Boston sports teams a challenging question. Now this young man could only answer through a computer assisted communication device, which he had mastered despite his disability. The question was: "if you could only have one day without your disability, and given your love for your Boston teams, what sport would you like to do: baseball, playing for the Red Sox, football, playing for the Patriots, basketball, playing for the Celtics, hockey, playing for the Bruins or what?" The young man looked at the interviewer and communicated a thoughtful answer and typed, using his breath to type each key. He said if he could do anything for just one day, it would be to "take my father for a run." Thinking about that interview these many years later, he would openly cry at that response. After a good cry, he would acknowledge the fact that the answer was what motivated his desire to do a triathlon and finish. One thing about Jack was that whatever he started, he would finish.

A full-length triathlon, or what many refer to as a full Ironman is a race in which competitors race first in a 2.4 mile swim, then ride a bicycle for 112 miles and finally run 26.2 miles to the finish. The races would be just like the race at Kona. Oh, by the way, it all must be done in 17 hours or less. For those who are not doing this sport for a living, that is an overwhelming objective. At his age most men will ride around a golf course in a golf cart hoping to finish in about 4 hours. This event is powered, not by an electric battery or gasoline powered engine but by your legs and arms in 17 hours or less, the equivalent of 4 rounds of golf by time.

Our hero, about to tackle his latest full length triathlon in the open waters of an extension of the Chesapeake Bay, is Jack Stone, and it is 2008 and the place is Cambridge, Maryland. Jack is accompanied by his wife Kate and they are from a small town in Pennsylvania outside of Philadelphia. Jack had retired from STAR Oil Company a few years before and had latched on a goal to do a full Ironman race annually. While he seemed obsessed, Kate supported this latest athletic endeavor, always celebrating his finishes, no matter how fast or slow. Jack knew swimming would be the toughest obstacle. It always would be. He had run many marathons and had taken up biking with his friend Dag who had been his running buddy for years until Dag's knees told him biking would be easier on his body. Dag had formed a small bike group that charted out bike routes in eastern Pennsylvania that had to have two criteria: lots of hills and a place to stop midride for a Cup of Joe. After a few years of riding the Pennsylvania hills, Jack had convinced himself that if he just could do the swim, his triathlon goal would be achievable. Oh, he had competed on the swim team in high school, usually in races less than 100 yards. Someone had to finish last! Usually, he had been placed in the races just to fill out the field, just a competitor in lane 6. He had done some swimming long in the past when he was under fire and he had done countless practice swims and triathlon races, but swimming an Ironman race was always something else. It was an Ironman race and no matter how many races or practice swims he had done, the swim in an Ironman was just different.

CHAPTER 2— PRACTICE SWIM DAY BEFORE THE RACE

Kate had said goodbye as he had left the hotel room to ride his bike to the water, carrying his gear to make a complete workout that morning. He has pedaled through Cambridge to the banks of the Choptank, looking east across the water. The water is serene from his view. But it is always that way near the shore. It is early in the morning of a fall day and there is absolutely no wind; the sky is somewhat blue as the sun begins to rise. The Choptank is a small river that drains the Eastern Shore of Maryland into the Chesapeake Bay. The current is not very fast but is affected greatly by the wind and the tidal changes caused by the Chesapeake. Those winds make the Chesapeake one of the most popular sailing destinations on the East Coast of the Country. Those winds that toy with large sailing craft have been known to alter the normal flow of the Choptank dramatically. Local lore has it that decades ago a freak wind reversed the flow of the Choptank back towards the fishing and recreational town of Cambridge flooding the better part of the Eastern Shore. But this morning all is calm, and the cool morning was going to be great for a last practice a week before the annual triathlon, this year's ironman length race which would start yards from where he was standing. There were a few souls already in the smooth waters of the Choptank, gently swimming out and back, testing the current, the tidal influences and visualizing where the race markers were expected to be a week later. This morning the river was dotted with anchored craft ranging from small to large, sailboats to small cabin cruisers to large yachts, still secured this late in the season. Soon, many would be housed in secure berths or inside sheltered storage warehouses. Where they were now anchored, they offered sighting targets and estimated ranges for the swimmers. But the silent swimmers had to avoid getting too close to the boats this early in the day. Some of the vessels were preparing to launch from their mooring point into the main channel of the Choptank and then to the Chesapeake for a fishing outing on what promised to be an uneventful day.

Weather forecasting was always a mathematical science. As the prevailing winds in the country moved west to east, information was shared west to east of actual weather reports allowing further eastern forecasters to "predict" weather over the next few days. That worked well for decades until the computers took over and made weathermen and women look like geniuses. Many local news station personalities became media stars starting out as weather forecasters. In parts of the East Coast far from major news outlets, the weather was less predictable.

As he gazed out into the eastern sky before sunrise, he again thought that this might just be a bridge too far. Maybe he could do it but first he needed to convince himself that the water was just a step along the way. He was not a person that did this for a living, although Kate frequently mentioned that his training days for this event were sometimes longer than his former job at STAR. At his age most men were riding around a golf course in a golf cart. Few walked and fewer even carried their own golf bags. Four hours is the desired time and even with a cart that was difficult to do. This event is powered, not by an electric battery or gasoline powered engine but by your legs and arms in 17 hours or less, the equivalent of 2 full work days when working at STAR. But if you cannot make the swim cutoff, which is about 2 hours and 15 minutes, you were out. You were done. All that training was wasted.

What makes the swim so hard, you might ask. Well, if you judge the sport by watching the long-distance swimmers in the Olympics, you might conclude that it is effortless and an event that allows one to glide through the water, casually breathing from time to time. Well, certainly the Olympic greats make the swim look easy and effortless. It just isn't. And Jack knew it from the very beginning. Jack had swimming experience from high school. Big deal! He often thought about those high school swim meets and that swim team. That team had sent two swimmers to the 1968 Olympics in Mexico City. But swimming laps beside two future Olympians is like walking along a horse racetrack while Secretariat was racing by on the turf. Just not the same. Jack was just a guy in lane 6 in those races. Besides, Jack outweighed the typical Olympic swimmer by nearly 60 pounds and had legs with pounds of muscle but no innate buoyancy. His arms were not his core asset and probably never would be. In short, his nickname would have been the "Rock", if that name had not already been taken. So, the best he could hope for would be to finish the Ironman length swim under the time limit for that segment of the race. In fact, his coach Bill House had recognized the shortcomings of his mentee and tailored Jack's workouts to endure the time in the water. But if the physical limits weren't daunting enough, imagine slogging away for 2 hours hearing little, seeing less and hoping you were going the right direction following floating inflated markers that became visible only 25 or 50 yards away. Counting them would be one of the few diversions during the first leg of the event. Dodging your fellow competitors bumping into you in the water was another.

In addition to the physical challenges of weight, lack of buoyancy, and limited strength, would be the water itself. Courses differed dramatically from another because of the temperature of the water. If too warm, you might find jellyfish stinging your arms, legs and face. If it was very cold, like an early season race might be, the temperature of the body of water might be in the low 60's. In fact some water would be so cold, it was like a getting slapped in the face. Of course, for old guys like Jack who were not professional racers, where water temperatures were less than 75 degrees, buoyant wetsuits were permitted to be worn. Salt water would be a bonus, but typically racecourses in saltwater bodies were influenced greatly by wave action and the current. And some of these swim courses, depending on the time of year might not be cool enough to provide the participants with the benefit of cool water for a wetsuit swim and the buoyancy of the salt water. So racers were choosy about their races. River courses could be really beneficial if the course was down stream, swimming with the current of 1 to 3 miles per hour would give even the poor swimmers a hope to actually finish the swim. But diabolic race directors seemed to come up with ways the make the course challenging by throwing in a half mile of upstream swimming in the race design. It clearly spreads the field out but makes the swim portion of the race most challenging.

The race on the Choptank would be unlike some of the races Jack had done. It was a combination of partial saltwater and river flow from the Eastern Shore of Maryland towards the Chesapeake Bay and the tidal influences of that Bay into which the Choptank emptied. And the wind, oh my God, how the wind could take a calm body of water like the seemingly protected race course and turn it into the backdrop for a play like the "Tempest." If the wind blew in from the West at the same time the tidal flow came in from the Chesapeake, you could be swimming an extra 20 minutes just trying to get through the last 100 yards of the swim to the exit.

Yes, Jack knew all of this as he looked over the dark water of the Choptank from his position on the old swing set in the park on the edge of the bank that stood next to the entry into the swim start. He had analyzed the historic water temperatures, the typical tidal times and other factors in making his choice for this upcoming event. He had talked with an old timer that after years of racing had convinced himself that, if he could not use his wetsuit, he would not race at all. Jack in talking through this seemingly irrational position with his buddy, understood clearly how psychology affected racers. It was not enough to be well trained; you could not have negative thoughts on your mind. It just makes a difference if you are replaying the theme of the "little engine that could" in your mind instead of "Holy Shit, I will never, ever, ever, make it through the swim!" But today Jack was feeling the good vibes. The water was calm, the tides were favorable, the water temperature was perfect and just a few race participants were practicing. This course was going to be two laps approximately a mile each with about a quarter of a mile to the finish exit. The trick for the slow folks would be to swim the first lap fast enough so that the faster swimmers did not crawl over them as they were well into their second lap. Collisions do happen and us slow pokes have been known to be injured by the faster folks or even the rescue kayakers intervening to rescue a swimmer in trouble. No one thinks they will drown but it does happen. So you just have to be prepared for anything. Jack snapped out of it. Enough negative thoughts! This was just a practice swim.

With all these things swirling through his mind, Jack looked back into the far reaches of the park that overlooks the swim course and spots an unusual tent. This was no typical REI camping tent. It was something directly out of a scene from Lawrence of Arabia. It was huge. And it was surrounded by several sentries that were walking around the tent, eyes darting left and right. While they may have been armed, they were so intimidating that they did not have to be. The more he observed this strange scene, the more curious he became. As he continued to wonder what this was all about, two men emerged from the tent while the sentries began to converge on them. It was still well before dawn and barely light enough to make out who these strange people were. But one thing was clear, this was someone special, requiring security, at least the sentries acted that way. Still the sentries gave the two figures some space and Jack could begin to see them better with the backdrop of the light from the tent and the many swimmers to be that were walking around the area waiting to get started on their practice swim holding small flashlights to mark their way. The figure on the left was drawing all the attention from the sentries. He stood well over 6 feet, was bearded and was wearing, what looked from where Jack was standing, a green and gold colored Tri Suit. Basically, a Tri Suit it is a onesie covering the upper torso as well as the butt and thighs. It provides limited buoyancy but does tend to keep the body streamlined and somewhat warm in the water. The male on the right was shorter, perhaps 5'8" or so. He too was wearing an identical colored Tri Suit. Jack concluded that the taller man must be some dignitary, perhaps a member of some royal family from a middle eastern country. Jack watched as the tall figure eased into the water alongside the figure accompanying him. As they entered the water he gave the smaller figure another look. Then it came to him. He realized, "I know this man." It was a long time ago. As he thought on this man, he ran back the years to the Beginning.

CHAPTER 3 — THE BEGINNING

Jack had reported for his first day of work at his first job as a recently graduated lawyer and had taken the PA Bar Exam. Jack and 4 other newbies were summoned into a conference room at the headquarters of STAR Oil Company. Jack thought that all would be congratulated on their accomplishments and be assigned coveted offices and shown around the company headquarters. WRONG! Jack and the others were greeted by the Chief Administrator for HR Constance Newbold and the Chief Corporate Attorney Jason George. The attorney sitting next to Jack murmured that both Constance and Jason were related to the family that controlled STAR. That was beyond Jack's control as he was just happy to have one of the few jobs available to attorneys desiring to enter the corporate world. He was the first in his family to finish college and being a law school graduate had left his parents over the moon. Those accomplishments made little difference to Jason. Jason began to speak: "First, if you have not already done so, let me introduce you to each other: Jack Stone is from Villanova Law, with a brief tour in the National Guard before graduating; Andy Braun, recently graduated from NYU Law, with an undergraduate degree in earth sciences; Steve Baron, a graduate from Temple after having served this country for three years in Viet Nam; Doug Moore, graduate of UVA Law with an undergraduate degree in mechanical engineering; and George Cook, a recent graduate of the University of Pennslvania Law School, with an undergraduate degree majoring in accounting. You five represent the best class of lawyers we have ever hired, based on your credentials. However, you should know that your class is the last eligible for our internal management training program. Corporations had historically trained middle and upper management employees upon entry into the company and our corporate legal staff has successfully lobbied for inclusion of our entry level lawyers in this program. Ironically, you are the first to be included in a program that will be ending. But you will get the best of a great program that has been improved over the years of its existence. You will be exposed to a business unit, its practices and procedures for the next six months in order to better prepare you as counselors to that unit and eventually to others. You will learn how the business is run; what its risks are; what the regular 'Joe' does day to day in that business unit; in short you will be part of the operation. If this scares you, there is the door. Leave now! But you will regret it; nowhere else in the country will you get to experience how a business is run from the ground up. In years to come, the business managers you deal with will appreciate how well you understand the pressure they are under and the risks they deal with from day to day. You will know when you can take what your client says at "face value" and when you can handle the real truth of the situation facing your client. What you learn over the next six months will be part of your legal DNA. Sure, we could just issue you legal pads with your name on them and give you a fancy desk. But I think, if you can handle it, you will find that in six months, you will be among the finest corporate attorneys in this industry." Wow, Jack thought, this will be an awesome adventure. It was more than the corporate recruiter described when he interviewed at Villanova.

Next Constance outlined the five businesses that had openings: gasoline marketing; corporate finance; oil and gas exploration; oil refining; and shipbuilding and transport. She then asked them to indicate which one they would be interested in. Jack jumped on the shipbuilding and transport, George, corporate finance; Andy, exploration; Doug refining and Steve, gasoline marketing. Constance said, "Having heard no conflicting interests, assume your requests a given." Over the first two weeks of general emersion in the business of STAR, Jack and the others were deemed ready to enter the program. During that time, they were locked on campus, living in the corporate dorms and taking their meals in the training center. It was amazing how quickly they had absorbed the materials and learned about each other. They would become as close to family they would know in STAR. They sometimes called themselves the "newbies."

It was now in the late fall of 1979 and the world had gotten over the sudden departure of the Shah of Iran, the weak civil government awaiting the assumed arrival and installation of a theocratic government led by the Allatolah Khomeini. Jack had been brought up to date by the STAR international planners of the relevance of STAR's decade long relationship with Iran. First, STAR's refineries were configured to run on Iranian crude which increased production of gasoline with less residual products, yielding lower priced by-products; and Second, STAR's international oil and gas exploration unit had invested during the Shah era in several oil concessions that had great potential. The reality of the relationship assured STAR that it would have access to sales of Iranian crude, certainly as long as the exploration efforts continued. From the Iranian government's view during the reign of the Shah, the opportunity for large exports of crude would drive oil companies to invest in proven exploration properties. Thus, whoever was the highest bidder in exploration opportunities could be in the best position to obtain huge contracts to purchase crude oil. But oil companies also realized that transporting oil in small tankers across the Atlantic was dramatically more expensive than building super large vessels capable of carrying 3-5 times more petroleum cargo. So their pitch to Iran was that we can make this work for us if we can get our large tankers into ports in Iran and sell the production, once it comes on stream to one of our affiliate companies. We can be a good partner, benefit the Iranian economy by taking more production per tanker while the exploration work was being undertaken. If Iran developed its port facilities in the near term, it would open up their exports to the highest bidder. This would be a "win win" propostion for the bidders for the exploration leases. Building tankers was in vogue again. This improved the bottom line of those companies with an eye on the future. STAR was one of these companies. However, Iran desired to have a mix of oil companies involved in the exploration effort so that the major oil companies did not control future production and sales of crude. STAR was prepared to be just a purchaser of crude oil and let others take the risks of exploration. But STAR was urged by US Government officials to participate in the bidding for exploration properties to blunt the argument that big American

Companies were going to dominate the exploration for oil in Iran. So STAR joined a group of smaller companies including Pacific Oil Company and Calhoon Exploration to explore for oil and gas. At the time, of the award of the bids, the belief was mixed: one view was that the Shah and his family would rule into the future and even if they did not, the US and European Countries could still control the future as they had in the past and find a worthy successor that would be pro Western and not aligned with Russia. Either way, the US Government and the advisors to the major oil companies felt, Iran was a safe place to invest. The US Government and the so called experts were no better at predicting the future than they were in the Far East or Venezuela. Maybe this favorable view of the future was reasonable at the time but all the investing oil companies seemed to share this optimistic view of the future. A clear reading of the then present climate in the world was that the oil and natural resources of every country belonged to that country. The oil to be found by an American Company in a foreign country was not "American Oil" but oil of that foreign country, subject to contractual undertakings that were subject to change. If the country acted unfairly or arbitrarily, there were well known ways of assuring fair treatment for the contracting parties. But the overarching reason the US Government felt Iran was the place to be is simple. The Shah was their guy. The CIA had plotted to have him placed in power defeating a coup and the Government had supported him for nearly two decades. Little wonder why there was so much anti-US sentiment in Iran.

Jack found himself, after a month of shorter voyages between Puerto Rico and the US, on the largest tanker in the STAR fleet, the Yabucoa, heading to Iran to obtain what would be the largest purchase of Iranian crude ever made by STAR. Despite the bumpy relationship caused initially by the departure of the Shah, the Iranian Oil Company had managed to reliably deliver on their crude contracts. But as Jack had learned from Doug, his fellow newbie, not every cargo purchased for STAR's refineries was processed by STAR. Sometimes the cargo would be sold during, or even before transit. In a rapidly rising crude market, a cargo might be sold several times before it reached its destination, and the destination itself could change depending on the transaction. Iranian crude purchased by an American oil company might never be processed in America. Europe could well be the eventual destination.

Much had changed in Iran since the exploration contracts were inked by Iran's National Oil Company, on behalf of Iran, Iran and the consortium of STAR, Pacific Oil Company and Calhoon Oil Company. Calhoon, within months of signing had opted to forfeit its interest and conveyed it equally to STAR and Pacific Oil. The risks were high and the investment more than Calhoon could handle. STAR and Pacific were more bullish. But the entire world was changing. Just a few years earlier, Venezuela had asserted its sovereignty over its natural resources and effectively terminated the oil and gas production rights of various US and European companies. That was subject to litigation through international arbitration. Other countries were examining whether the basic exploration agreements and the rights to control the oil that might eventually be produced under those contracts were fair to the countries. If the countries were under the influence of the US Government or major European countries and the oil companies were major players in those countries, was it possible, dissidents argued, that the basic exploration and production agreements were not as fair as they should be. Iranians dissidents were claiming that their leaders, in particular the Shah was guilty of corruption and that he was under the control of the West. Something had to be changed. The Iranian people, these dissidents argued, were not seeing the full benefit of the sale of their natural resources. Of course, this was not necessarily the only driver of the attempt to end the Shah's regime, but it was easy to calculate and provided a secular reason to add to the religious battle for the people of Iran. Belief that the Shah would come back to power was just out of the question and photos of the clearly ill Shah along with rumors of his terminal cancer were pretty convincing.

After a cruise of nearly 20 days, the tanker Yabucoa, had approached the Iranian port of Kharg Island, docked and would begin the loading process that day. Kharg Island was one of the major port facilities built to induce the oil companies to invest in building large tanker vessels. Whether Iran, the investors in the terminal or the oil companies owning these large tankers would reap the benefits of the arrangement would be left to the future. That future was looking pretty shaky now. But by the time the ship had arrived, the world had changed. The Shah had since fled the country and what elected officials remained to keep the government running were completely ineffective and had invited the Allatolah Khomeini to return from Paris where he had been in exile.

Kharg Island would be where the Yabucoa would dock. The captain and crew had been following the events in Iran and communicating with Headquarters continuously throughout the voyage. Jack had been an attentive listener during the voyage. Jack had been asked by Jason George to see if he could disembark during the loading process and travel to the STAR exploration site some 70 miles from the port. There he was to take delivery of the latest geological reports that would provide data on the efforts to date. That information might be the basis for broadening the exploration efforts or even finding another investor to take a portion of STAR'S investment. Jack had arranged several days ahead of arrival to secure a small motorboat with a pilot and a motor bike once he was on the mainland. He had obtained proper directions to the STAR exploration field offices from the Yabucoa crew. Remember paper maps were the norm in that day and age. After sailing from Kharg Island to the mainland, Jack cleared the security and passport checkpoints. He picked up the motorbike and observing that it must have been built a decade before, he set off. Assured that this was the best he could do, he took off North following the map and the verbal directions from the crew of the Yabucoa. The journey was dusty and hot and after a two hour ride he neared the fence line surrounding the STAR facilities. Jack noted that he had ridden nearly 75 miles or so from the port. The field offices were well over 300 miles from the City of Tehran. Yet as he approached the property, there seemed to be hundreds of civilians gathered outside the fence line. These were young protestors, mostly college aged kids really, with signs in Farsi, the Iranian language. They were chanting for Americans to go home. Clearly, they had been convinced that American companies were treating Iran unfairly and were advocating for the Iranian government, whoever would be running it to throw the American companies out. Ironically, many of the workers inside the gate were Iranian Nationals at whom the protestors were directing their chanting. While he could not understand the Farsi language on the signs, it was clear from the chants that the likelihood of future investment in exploration efforts was a pipe dream as long as this type of protest continued. It was also clear that no one would pay a dime to step into STAR'S shoes in whole or in part facing this kind of turmoil. Jack was less concerned with the future of the leases that his own well-being. These protestors were not attending a political rally. This was approaching an attack on the facilities. People could be hurt, possibly lives could be lost. Jack discreetly entered the gate without drawing any attention and went directly to the Superintendent's office. Durbert Hughes, the Superintendent, greeted Jack and said, "Thanks for making the trip from the ship but we haven't much time. I have just received word, unofficially of course, that the US Embassy in Teheran is likewise under siege with thousands of more protestors. They intend to seize the Embassy or at least provoke an armed response from the guards. My sources of information say the Iranian Government has officially declared all foreign workers in the country after today *"persona non grata"* and ordered them to be deported if they do not leave immediately. The order further declares that the oil fields are to be seized forthwith. Here are copies of the reports your boss requested, a list of US personnel here at our offices, a schedule of all equipment, assets and funds spent to date. I am shutting down operations immediately and evacuating all non-Iranian personnel to Iraq. Get on the bike and leave! Now get!" All Jack could do was nod and say, "yes sir."

Jack threw the files and reports in his backpack and jumped on the bike and quickly exited the front gate. The bike made so much noise that he could not tell if he was hearing gunfire or backfire from the bike as he exited. As he tore towards the exit he found a young protester blocking his exit. He got a quick look at the youth's face, clean shaven and dressed in a white, loose-fitting garb. The youth said nothing but leaned toward him and grabbed his backpack and then let it go. Jack sped off and as he looked back he could see that the protestors had stormed the fence. They were in the process of trying to stop the vehicles exiting out the side gates of the compound with the field workers. The youth had begun to walk towards the crowd of protesters and disappeared into the crowd.

He needed to communicate with the Headquarters and quickly. But first he had to coax the ancient motorbike to the port over 2 hours away. As he chugged along, the thought occurred to him that the ship must have been alerted to the protests and attack on the oil facilities. Further, there was no guarantee that the protests would not occur at the port either. As he neared the port he could see smoke in the distance. Was it fire? Was it some kind of explosions? He could not tell. What if the ship had left him behind? Perfectly logical that the ship's captain would sacrifice a young lawyer over having his vessel seized by protestors or even Iranian officials. As he drew closer, he saw a large group of protestors gathering near the entrance to the dock where he had left the motor boat. Indeed there were fires burning in empty oil barrels but no bombs and no shooting. That was a relief. Again, the signs they held were in Farsi, which he could not read. He slipped around the protestors and untied the line and jumped in carrying the backpack, leaving the pilot behind. He had cut his teeth driving motorboats like this during the summers vacationing in the Pennsylvania lakes in the Poconos. Surely, he could make it to the tanker before it sailed. As he approached Kharg Island, he saw that the ship had begun easing away from the loading platform and was picking up speed. He was screwed!

He sped up with hopes that he could make it to the ship, attract the crew's attention and get on board somehow. Racing as fast as the motorboat could go, he looked down in the cabin and saw a large plastic trash bag that was used by the pilot to dispose of trash. Steering the boat with one hand, he grabbed the plastic bag with the other. He pulled it loose and opened his backpack, dumped the contents into the plastic bag and placed it back into his backpack. He threw the backpack over his shoulders and kept on going. Just as the motorboat seemed to draw closer to the Yabucoa, it began to cough. Nuts, he thought, there might not be enough fuel to make it. Holding on to the wheel and keeping the throttle wide open, he began to take off his shoes and pants. He had been traveling over a mile from Kharg Island and by now the tanker was really picking up speed. The motorboat was shutting down and Jack, having no other choice, jumped into the water and began dog paddling after the ship. After 10 seconds, he realized that "this was crazy." He had not swum since High School and then his longest competition then was 100 yards. The ship was kicking ass to depart but many of the crew were on the railing looking aback at the port, and suddenly one must have spotted Jack jumping into the water from the motor boat and making for the ship. The crewman shouted up to the bridge that a person was struggling to make for the ship. The captain had received his orders to get out of Dodge ASAP and he was doing just that. Whoever it was, it did not matter. This cargo must not be jeopardized. But then he remembered the young lawyer that had left the ship this morning. Could it be him? He hit the intercom and instructed the crew to launch the rescue launch ASAP and see if it possibly was Jack. The captain knew he was taking a big risk and putting those involved in lowering the launch in harm's way while the ship was gathering speed. But the captain understood the reality. If the Iranian government wanted to stop his ship, they had armed vessels that could head him off or capture his ship. It might be a close call, but his conscience at least would be clear. If that was Jack, he had to get him on board. He was leaving no one behind. He split the difference and opted to send a rescue party and slowed the ship down a bit.

The launch closed on the struggling Jack after he had been swimming for what seemed an hour but was no more than 30 minutes. Despite the effort Jack had covered only about 150 yards and was barely treading water at that point. Yes, the crew in the launch observed, this idiot was the lawyer that the captain had told them to rescue. He might be an idiot, but they had all come to know Jack well during the voyage to Iran. He was one of them and they would rescue him if they could. Crewman at the bow of the launch threw Jack a rescue ring and yelled out that Jack should just grab it and hold on to it while they came about. They hauled him aboard and immediately set course to rendezvous with the ship now nearly 2 miles ahead. Jack checked his backpack to make sure that the contents were safe when he noticed that two capsules about the size of to go cups of coffee had been inserted in the side pockets of the backpack. Didn't have a clue what they were but thought that the air inside had probably helped to keep him afloat. As they drew near the ship, Jack thought: someday, I will swim a mile easily, but not today.

CHAPTER 4 — THE CLAIM

Onboard, Jack, after profusely thanking the captain for not leaving him to drown or be captured by the student protestors, retired to the conference room which was next to the communications center of the ship. He began to put together a communiqué to the corporate offices and a series of messages to the fellow class of newbie lawyers that were taking similar assignments. The first was to Andy, now having direct access to the VP of exploration, alerting him that the exploration fields were in the process of being seized and probably all foreign workers were either expelled or were going to be. He contacted Doug, now working directly with the VP of refining. He said that the ship had pulled out of port and was heading for the Suez Canal. He said that the vessel had, according to the bill of lading, a million barrels of Iranian Crude and that payment was due 30 days hence. Jack questioned whether that payment had to be made at that time. He expressed his view that maybe it should not be paid at all, if it was true that the oil fields had been expropriated. Lawyers with more seasoning would have to opine on that and advise the proper course. But Jack felt that if the Iranian government had taken the oil fields, paying for the oil being transported on this very vessel would be plainly stupid. And after nearly drowning, he would cry to high heaven if anyone in legal would suggest that payment be made. But as Jack came to see later, this was not an easy question for the lawyers, and more importantly, not for the business units. When Jack got back to STAR'S Philadelphia refinery, he turned in the files in his back pack to be forwarded to Jason's office. It was not until several years later that the information on those documents would be used in the Iranian litigation. As for the tubes he had carried that had helped on his swim, he had kept them unopened and sealed. No one asked for them. So, he just held on to them, souvenirs of a ride through Iran.

A week after he arrived at the home port, Jack learned that STAR'S executives were still considering what to do with the situation. The payment date was nearing and questions were being raised about the legality of even running the crude through the refinery system. The trading arm of STAR had attempted to sell the crude repeatedly during the voyage in order to pass the problem on to someone else, anyone else. The US Government gave absolutely no guidance on the rights of a purchaser of crude from Iran, even one that was taken into possession at a time that was perfectly legal and proper. Compounding the problem was that the US Government implemented a series of actions that at times raised more problems than it solved. First, an embargo on Iranian crude was put into place (but it failed to specifically exempt or address crude acquired at the time of the Iranian incident giving rise to the embargo). This made the sale of the crude to a third party a problem but it clarified the situation somewhat; Second, all funds of Iran in any financial institution were subject to a freeze, meaning that if a US Company that had payments due from Iran were unable to legally receive the funds without US approval (good luck if you wanted to see any funds for years). Third, funds to be paid to Iran for goods and services were blocked without a specific approval of the US Government. While this clarified what STAR could do with the funds due from the lifting of the cargo by the Yabucoa, it did not require payment to the account. Of course, payments could be made to the frozen accounts of Iran. Interest rates were still high at the time and STAR financial personnel reasoned that even with high interest rates, STAR could do better investing the funds in the business that any interest rate they would have to pay to Iran in the future. The price of crude on the open market soared immediately with the seizure of the fields and the implementation of sanctions and the embargo. Holding onto the crude and not paying for it seemed to be the prudent course of action.

But a company like STAR would be affected by the entire pressure on the international crude market. Prices went up at a faster pace than they could be rolled through the refining arm of the company. Domestic gasoline, heating oil and jet fuel pricing all soared. Companies without a balance between exploration and production and refining were in a bind. Jack and his network of newbie lawyers understood very well the shock that was about to roll through the company. One of the biggest barriers to success was the lingering price controls that had been put into place to protect the consumers complaining about high gasoline prices. That meant that rolling through spiking crude prices to the gasoline pump proved to be problematic. While price controls were being eliminated, the Congressional investigations relating to price gouging were just getting started. Break up the oil companies was the theme of the day. The companies took less risk and purchased less international crude in an effort to push the markets toward a surplus. Price of domestic crude had long been tied to the international crude market. So reliability of supply could be solved but the price of crude just went up. Collaborating among the oil companies to accomplish lower pricing was of course illegal. Chaos then reigned with the predicable lines of cars forming at the pump as inventory was reduced. Companies began to dust off old reports of domestic crude oil fields that had been either abandoned or lacked justification to invest in ways to increase production. All through this economic reaction to the population of one country to overthrow an unpopular leader, diplomacy had no chance of addressing some resolution when the students attacked the US embassy in Tehran and captured over 300 personnel. When the Iranian government, that was not on good terms with anyone, failed to intervene and the hostage crisis lingered on beyond a year, the possibility of a resolution and restoration of good relationships between countries was forever lost. Decades later, no one in the US government could get over the hostage crisis and its ramifications. And further, anyone that appeared to be the least conciliatory towards Iran was subject to criticism and condemnation or worse.

It was in the midst of all this turmoil that a strategy was suggested by several of the "newbie" lawyers and run up the flagpole of the legal department: first, hold on to the cash for the crude-don't pay it to Iran or to the financial institutions where Iranian funds were being held; second, use the cash to bridge the crisis; third, run the crude through the refinery system knowing that the gasoline and other by-products increased in value hourly; fourth, put together a claim against Iran for taking the oil fields and wait until a clear process was available to sue for damages for the taking and if such a claim could be presented use the claim as a basis for not paying for the crude. The legal structure of the advice was critical as it put rationale to the kneejerk reactions that the business units might do anyway. Moreover, the financial markets were looking keenly at STAR to make sure that the treatment of liabilities and income were proper and legally sound. Executives would be expected to stand before analysts and even the US government and declare, "we know what we are doing; it is right and legally proper; we will fight for what is due us; and we will prevail" If we are the only company doing it this way, tough, the lawyers argued. Early on STAR'S financial staff identified that for reporting purposes, unlike the legal niceties of being able to offset a payment with a claim, if there is any possibility of not prevailing on the claim, the payment had to be booked. If the Iranians could reasonably make a claim for principal and interest, then interest at the then current rate had to be booked as well. And so it was, with copious footnotes describing how the company would prevail and why the investors should view the company as worth what the financials above the line indicated. A lot of hours and sweat went into that position and the simple footnote to the financial reports and the words stayed in place for nearly a decade. The basis for a claim was there and the value of it would take years to quantify. But the consultants and Investment Bankers, who always sensed a fee to be earned, even if real value were not created, began chanting to the STAR Board and to its principal shareholders, the whole company was worth more separately than as a single entity.

CHAPTER 5 — DEALS AND LIFE

Jack and his newbies emersed themselves in various parts of STAR, watching as the company seemed to be listening to the Investment Bankers and possibly going the route of Bell and AT&T. STAR had anticipated the legal threat of being broken up into pieces and created smaller entitles that were semi autonomous for a few years by then. This strategy was excellent for developing the future generations of leadership within the company. Less experienced managers were handling responsibilities far above their paygrade. While their understanding of their business unit was perfected, it also created a few problems. Independence of these various divisions or organizations, well in advance of super integrated accounting systems and the era of zoom calls and the like, created an atmosphere of fiefdoms in which individuals in charge could possibly enrich their business unit at the expense of the entire enterprise. It also made the auditors focus on the possibility of conflicts of interest and personal gain from sticky fingers. But more importantly the collaboration necessary to benefit the entire conglomerate was lost in battles between which organization benefitted in a particular transaction that bridged one or more subsidiary. More importantly, the newbies were handed opportunities to do major transactions in the line of business that the companies were in. While experience would be developed doing these deals, there were other experiences they would have. Creating separately run businesses with profit and loss responsibilities could create "hero" decisions. Executives were driven to attempt to amass profits or find unique business opportunities. Sometimes this would lead to bizarre results as business leaders would jump on opportunities that one could even call scams. Judgment at times was lost seeking to be a hero. Here is one that Jack heard about. A vendor contacted a subsidiary business leader and made a pitch that his company had a device developed in his garage that could find precious minerals simply by sending a signal down from a flying object, such as a airplane or helicopter, to the ground. Once the signal would rebound, it would be able to indicate the presence of precious minerals. The vendor convinced the business manager it could find uranium, gold, copper and any other mineral you can think of that is hard to find in large quantities. Well, if it sounds too good to be true, it probably is. In any event this business leader not only commissioned the vendor to proceed but had organized a top secret effort by hundreds of agents to swarm counties in three states to lock up long term leases that would cover any mineral discovered. Jack just shook his head as he reviewed the reports. Nothing was ever found. The reports of this endeavor were buried and lost. STAR would not become a golden company.

But the newbies really cut their teeth on acquisitions over the next 5 years. Then for the balance of the decade, they worked on divestments or sales of the various businesses they had worked on to purchase. Being flexible was a good quality to have that decade. They developed their drafting skills writing and negotiating provisions that assured the deal would benefit the company as intended and protected the company when and if the deal went south. They not only honed these skills but spent the time talking with fellow newbies to pass on not only war stories but negotiating tips to use in the future. They each became in their own way not only great counselors but exceptional negotiators. The business leaders that worked with them all became better for their experiences working with any of the newbies. The predictions Jason made a decade before about becoming the finest corporate attorneys in STAR, was so true it was uncanny.

And then the inevitable came. Just as the Bell system was spun off to the public and became a ghost of its former self, albeit because of government edict, the financial vultures, the Investment Bankers finally convinced the executive team and more importantly, the principal shareholders, as well as the Board, that it was Time; Time for change; Time to split the company in two. The pieces of the pie were worth more than the pie itself. Each piece could not only survive without the other, but each would thrive. Once the select few that then steered the company were on board, it was clear that the company Jack and the newbies knew would be no more. The dream of the founding family came to an end. A new generation of the founding family had taken charge and intended to survive and prosper. That would unlikely be the case for many in the workforce that had helped make STAR what it had become.

It meant that Andy Braun would become the chief legal officer of the newly created EPOC(later to be called "Neptune"). Jack would be a senior legal guy along with Steve Baron, and Doug Moore. George Cook had transitioned to the finance side of the business and would be named CFO of EPOC. Maybe the three remaining with STAR would make it to retirement or they would reinvent themselves as George Cook had. It was time for Jack and the three members of the newbies still working for STAR to focus inwardly. Jack had taken up marathon running half way through the decade and began a quest to complete 30 marathons before 45. He set his sights on Boston, New York, Big Sur and the Marine Corps Marathon. Philadelphia had become his go to race.

Andy had always been interested in cycling. He would ride his bike 20 miles to work each day and back home in the evening. Racing bikes had become his passion also about half way through the decade. He began entering tortuous century races, rides like the Hilly 100 or the Ride Across America, a relay ride with six of his colleagues. He could endure the pain if the accomplishment was significant enough. You might think I exaggerate, but he fell leading off the first leg one of his 6 team rides from California to the Atlantic. The fall was caused by thorns from a beach bush which caused a flat. In the fall Andy fractured his hip. He refused to stop. Limited in his movements, he could endure the pain as long as he was peddling. He could not walk and he could not lift his leg over the saddle. He could only get on and off the bike for each of his 2-hour legs by laying the bike on the ground and sliding off to an air mattress that would be loaded into the team mobile home. He was a wreck; but he could pedal. He endured 10 days, religiously taking his 2-hour shift, day or night until the team reached the Atlantic. He finished the ride but spent a week in the hospital. It took eight screws to put the thighbone back together. He might not run but he was determined to resume biking one day. Jack always spoke of Andy's fete with great reverence long after the separation of the business units. He thought often, if Andy can do it, maybe I can accomplish something great. That drove him in part to run his races and his goal of 30 Marathons.

George Cook had spent the years retooling his academic focus, gotten an MBA from Temple and then a graduate degree in Tax. His investment in himself quickly propelled him through the financial ranks to the executive level. Although just as interested in physical activities as Jack or Andy, he felt that he needed to invest his time on his mind and that was enough. The rewards were inside the financial organization of the Company.

Doug Moore devoted his weekends, holidays and vacations to his growing real estate ventures at the NJ Shore, buying and refinishing homes and praying that costal storms did not wash away his nest egg. His wife and kids thrived in this lifestyle, becoming lifeguards, surfers and entrepreneurs centered on the shore. He moved on from surfing to open water swimming. He had followed Diana Nyaad's career and instantly became a fan. Although not an Olympic caliber swimmer, he felt the comfort of the ocean seemingly parting as he would glide through the waters. The races he began entering were sparsely attended by fans but he liked it that way. The courses were challenging but interesting. Ocean City to Atlantic City; Long Beach Island from Top to Bottom; Cape May to Rehoboth; Swim the Hudson (from the GW Bridge to Ellis Island. He even swam the swim portion of the "Escape from Alcatraz." Doug had done it all but now his interest was focused on spending time at the beach puttering around and fixing up his various beach homes he owned or co-owned with investors. Somehow, he still fit in his work at STAR. He had not caught the bug of promotion at all costs and was perfectly comfortable working as a key member of a legal team no matter what the issue.

Once it was clear that the decoupling was going to be a done deal and the submissions were prepared to be mailed to shareholders for approval, the remnants of the newbie 5 contacted one another. None except Andy had been in on the deal preparation but they knew they would be part of the implementation of the separation. And besides, they felt the need to keep in touch even if that was not the case. They thought a conference call would be the way to do it. Jack organized the call. They thought that a good way to kick it off was to discuss what was going on in their lives. How were the marriages going; were their kids finalizing college plans or playing competitive sports; what were their plans if the deal was followed with a downsizing plan. They covered the usual list of important events of life and how they were dealing with it. Towards the end of the call Andy said that he and Jack should talk about Iran after the call and by the way he said he had come across an interesting flyer about a new race taking place in Arizona, a full distance triathlon that would take place in six months, basically from Lake Powell to Scottsdale, Arizona. The organizers were looking for teams of three competitors that would have one member doing the swim leg, another bike well over a hundred miles and then the final member of the team would run a marathon. It would be the first time for the event and the tee shirts looked really cool. Jack and Doug said it was something to consider down the line. They finished the call on a high note and Jack promised to get back to Andy after the call. They all felt that life was good and that there would be life after and beyond the company. STAR was no longer going to be what it once was.

CHAPTER 6 — THE CALL

An hour flew by quickly. Jack had immediately looked into the topography and the climate challenges that the race that Andy had suggested might present. Even with three pretty fit guys splitting the distance between them, covering 140.6 miles over an open arid terrain with few spectators was a challenge not to be taken lightly. This was particularly true for the bike segment where a breakdown or hydration issue or even a missed turn might result in a permanently lost teammate. In a state where 100 degrees was a cool day, maybe, Jack thought, this might be more that a sane person should undertake. Maybe down the line. It was something he put in the back of his mind. As he was thinking about this, Andy called. "Thought you were going to call me back, Jack!" "Sorry, thinking about the challenges of a Scottsdale triathlon and got carried away." Jack said. Andy said, "the reason I wanted to talk is that I am sending you all our files on Iran overnight." Jack asked "Why. I thought that your spin off company was going to include the international exploration operations as well domestic exploration and production!" Andy replied, "Well that changed at the highest levels. STAR is going to keep the existing fields in Africa, the Middle East and Europe as well as all claims that were pending attributable to those areas. We will keep every other country we are in. Going on in the future, it is every company for themselves. But for now, the Iranian claim, the Libyan claim and the sticky wicket in Nigeria is your organization's obligation to handle. Oh, and that includes having to deal with the lawyers I was forced by your bosses to hire several years ago to pursue the claim against the Iranians. To date we have spent over $20 Million in legal fees, studies, travel expenses and arbitration fees. It's all in the files. You may wish that You never received the Iranian files. They are a mess but no more that the issues in the case. One more thing. Watch your back. Friends may be your enemies and enemies may prove to be your friends." Jack immediately replied, "What is that supposed to mean? I realize that this case has been going on as long as I have been here. Frankly, I have no involvement or detailed knowledge of how the case is being handled. I have not crossed swords with anyone about this. I realize that no one is happy spending huge sums of money with no return in sight. Why should I have to watch my back? I don't even know that the case will be my responsibility or even if I should raise my hand and volunteer to be involved." Andy said, "Look I have to sign off. I have said more than I was authorized to say at this point, except that no one in our organization has any knowledge about Iranian operations, the fields, the data, what went on at the time the exploration contracts were negotiated, or even why the fields were confiscated. All those personnel are either part of the few being transferred to STAR or retired and scattered to the wind. Sad to say that the outside lawyers know more about the facts than anyone else. The lawyers have all the names of the former employees and will share them with you if they choose." Jack said, "Wow! You know how to share information with just the right twist. Maybe, as big a profile case that this is, I am better off keeping my volunteering hand below the table." Andy concluded the call with the following: "There is no glory to be found in this case. I found that out. But I have done what I was directed to do. Please don't let this come between us."

Jack thought about the call for a bit as he sat in his office on the 10th Floor of his office on Walnut Street in downtown Philadelphia. This building had been owned by the company for 75 years before it was sold to a prominent real estate developer who had taken the historic executive offices and would convert them into a posh supper club and site of the ultra secret hermitage club which had ties to uber conservative organizations throughout the country. The lower floors had been leased back to the company as part of the inevitable cash raising efforts to equalize cash flows going forward as the Company sought out other businesses to explore outside the oil industry. He was housed in this building as the type of assignments he had been given over the past few years cut across company boundaries and it was easier to do the work from Philadelphia than out of the headquarters offices which were then situated in the suburbs. It was probably a good thing as rumor had it that the headquarters was would be relocating from the suburbs to Center City Philadelphia following the spinoff. Jack knew it would just be a matter of weeks before the entire management team, including lawyers and finance would be co-housed in some location, probably too small, and with fewer bells and whistles. He thought about going by train to the headquarters and talking with some of the finance guys as well as the legal executives, but he knew better. Sometimes a big secret is not so much so. When it was apparent that some kind of reorganization or deal was pending, the executive team frequently borrowed space in the legal offices of the Hamilton Burger firm which served as a shadow legal department of STAR and conducted the secret negotiations with investment bankers, lawyers and representatives of certain shareholders (meaning of course those that really controlled the strategic decisions of the company). That was where he expected to find who he was looking for. He approached the Ham building (as it was called by his fellow STAR lawyers) from the side and walked into the "Parisian Roaster", a café renowned for its French Roast Coffee and croissants. There he spotted just who he was looking for, Jason. Jason was sitting with the GC and the Managing partner of Hamiton Burger. He walked up to their table and interrupted their conversation. Jack said, "I don't mean to interrupt but I have something that I would like to bring to your attention immediately as it may affect what you are working on, whatever that is." Jason shook his hand and guided him to greet the others at the table who were Frank Peterson, the GC and Wellington Hughes the Managing Partner of Hamilton Burger and then said: "It is entirely inappropriate for you to be here. You are out of place and if you need to communicate with us, there is a well-established protocol for doing so and coming up to us in a public place uninvited is not within protocol." Jack was somewhat taken aback by Jason's statement but refused to back off. He said, "Look, I am perfectly aware that this is not the place for what I have to communicate but I have some information you need to hear and now. Can we move to a place where we can talk privately, NOW!" Jack was so forceful that the three lawyers looked at each other, nodded and got up and directed

Jack to a private room that obviously had been used by them over the past week as they had negotiated the separation of STAR from the exploration and production arm of STAR, then known as EPOC. Jason closed the door behind them but his body language reminded Jack of his next-door neighbor's Rottweiler growling and preparing to attack a would-be trespasser. Jack, sensing that Jason was going into attack mode lifted his arms slightly as if he was surrendering and said, "Look, I am not asking about what you are all negotiating if anything, and if what I am going to share with you is nothing, so be it. But a source from the exploration sub said that among other things that was being resolved between the organizations was that the Iranian claim would be our problem to deal with after any spinoff. My source said that this was viewed by the subsidiary as a windfall to them and that they were glad to be rid of it and finally, whoever would be handling it should be very cautious. Maybe in the scheme of things, this is a small concern but I felt you should be aware of the glee they have getting rid of the case." The three lawyers looked at him in disbelief, shock and silence. They neither acknowledged Jack's statement or contradicted it. Not seeing any response coming from the threesome, Jack backed out of the room and left to return to his office on Walnut Street. He did not expect a call from any of them to fill out a foursome that weekend at Merion Golf Club, maybe ever. He hoped that he still had a job at the end of the week. He hoped he had not gotten Andy into any trouble either.

A week later two things had happened: first, the deal, which had been first rumored, then confirmed by the public relations department internally to employees, at the time of the public filings and announcement that the deal was being submitted to the shareholders for approval. EPOC, the exploration and production company would be spun off and be named Neptune and STAR would not only be a refining and marketing company but also be responsible for current international operations in Europe, the Middle East and Africa. These would be evaluated over time and enhanced or disposed of as STAR saw fit. The entire press release focused on refining and marketing as well as logistics. International exploration was an afterthought. It might as well have been buried in a footnote. It was in the SEC filings, so it was not a secret. If the press release had footnotes, it would have been contained in one with the smallest print possible. Second, that afternoon, 15 boxes marked to Jack's attention arrived via Express FED, marked CONFIDENTIAL, TO BE OPENED BY THE ADDRESSEE ONLY. He had been handed the mess Andy had talked about.

It was clear to all the employees of STAR that this was a done deal. They had little say. The shares they owned would not matter to the vote. The major shareholder had been on board and all the financial investment houses rating the deal were drooling over the banking fees and commissions from sales by disgruntled shareholders and profit seeking shareholders bailing out. Thieir bottom lines would increase. Whether this would benefit employees in either Neptune or STAR remained to be seen. Despite the touting by the executive teams of both companies and the financial advisors that the separate parts had value far more than the company as a whole. Time would tell. Jack would not worry about that; he had to do something with the boxes that blocked his door. He contacted Jason immediately when the boxes had arrived and was instructed not to do a thing until the deal was approved. Then he should call and see if, when and where Jason and Frank Peterson could meet with him. Jack thought, another warm call! At least, he thought, he had a job until the deal was approved, maybe…

Jack began thinking back to that trip to Iran aboard the Tanker Yabucoa. That was how this had all begun from his perspective. Hard to believe that a single day had generated 15 boxes to resolve a claim. He still could not swim much more than 100 yards in a pool but that day, he had done that swimming for his life. He had survived. He would survive this too. In the corner of the office was the stained back pack that he had strapped to his body that day. It had moved with him from office to office from assignment to assignment across the country, wherever the company sent him. Kate would not let the backpack into his home. It wreaked of saltwater and oil. It reminded her of how close he had come to dying. She and Jack had married while Jack was in Law School and then in this first job, he had nearly drowned. She did not want to be reminded of that. It reminded him of that too, but it etched in his brain the need to finish what he started out to do; not to quit. That drive was part of his DNA. It drove him throughout his life. In every marathon he had competed in, he knew he could not finish first if he did not first finish. You had to finish the race. You had to finish.

The backpack drew him closer. He picked it up and thought. This is really older than almost anything in those boxes. As he picked up the backpack, he heard the metal canasters still in the side pocket clang together. Oh yea! Those damn canasters. I wonder. Ten years! Barely visible were the marks of the magic marker on the side of each marking the day he was pulled out of the water, celebrating the finish of his swim. But now after 10 years, the top of each canaster had slightly separated from the tube. Now what had before seemed to be solid pieces of metal had lids that could be removed. He opened one of the containers and pulled out a parchment like piece of paper rolled up like a scroll. It had writing on it, clearly in Farsi, along with numbers. He would have to find someone that could read this but now is not the time or place. Maybe another day. It probably had nothing to do with all these files sitting in the conference room next to his office, right? Well, if this is my case, I will find out the answer to that question.

CHAPTER 7 — THE CHAOS

As the deadline for the shareholder approval approached what heretofore, for STAR, had been a smooth-running ship, descended into chaos. Executive packages had been developed by HR as well as packages for regular rank and file employees, approved by the Board, were circulating. Downsize studies were presented, employees were evaluated and ranked. It was a horror show. The only ones to profit were the consultants that specialized in cutting costs. The mission was lost; programs to improve market position, increase sales were shit canned. The word "improved" was forever associated with the words "cost cutting measures." Outsourcing was the buzzword. Employees, managers and executives alike just treaded water, just as Jack had done a decade ago in the waters off Iran. It was a time for some to grab power and for even top executives to implement coups to improve positions. To make the whole downsizing go quickly and smoothly, the rumor mill worked its charms. The executives must have started some of these, if not encouraged their circulation. They never put out communiques that one rumor or another were completely false. Maybe they were clueless. One of these rumors which clearly pushed employees to raise their hands and self-select for a package within the deadlines was this: "whatever you see now is as generous as the company will be if it to do another reduction, it will not be voluntary. In fact, there may be no more than two weeks severance pay." Boy did that one rumor, never denied, stimulate people to raise their hands for the more generous voluntary severance package.

In the midst of all this, employees began to drop the dime on their managers, to out them for actions they had been taking that were improving their position at the expense of the company. Many of these were dumped into the laps of the lawyers. Some of managers who were outed probably could have been criminally prosecuted but weren't. There were too many; the publicity would have been ugly and it impeded the company's desires to just get rid of large numbers of people. In the end, reporting the bad actors did not save the whisperer's jobs. In the end, victims of bad managers went out the door along with the bad managers. But some of these left with the view that "if I have to lose my job, at least I know that my crook of a manager will be going too." The only consolation was that the bad manager was ineligible for the severance package and that the victims were. This was one of the most difficult periods Jack had experienced. He hoped it would end soon. Deep down he knew he would see it again. He saw that major companies were hiring former CEO's that specialized in downsizing nicknamed "Chainsaw" or the "Butcher." Headhunters were getting them stock options and major shares of a company to sign on to struggling companies. Growing the business was not going to land a successful executive a job with financial rewards.

The chaos affected every department, including the legal shop. Frank Peterson took the package and left moving on to Hamilton Burger, as of counsel, three assistant general counsel and six chief counsels were let go and, no surprise here, the new General Counsel was Jason. The day after the shareholder approval, the moment Jack showed up at the office from his run to work and shower he got a call from Jason's office. It was the executive secretary for the General Counsel who said, "Jack, hold on for General Counsel Jason George (as good a way as any to find out who your new boss was or who would be telling you that you were out of a job)." Jack held on for Jason and said: "Congratulations Jason, on the new job. Whatever I can do, let me know." Jason replied: "thanks, Jack. I want to talk about Iran for a moment if you have the time." "Sure" Jack replied. Jason continued: "Well, I want you to pick up the case and figure out what we need to do. As you may know, we had to book the costs of the case to date and a that is an immediate hit to the bottom line. Its small potatoes compared with the puts and takes of the whole spinoff but legal is being evaluated on expenses against budget and the fact that we are trying to recover money is disregarded. The Legal Department, as a general rule has no revenues. Costs recovered on a claim are just lumped in with all our defense costs we are spending. Recoveries just go to the business unit. The Legal department is continuously looked at by the Board and our CEO as a major identifiable expense. All we can do is spend less. Get this thing under control!" Jack could only nod. Jason continued, "But there are a couple of things you need to keep in mind: 1. You cannot change the law firm even if you were to find our counsel is charging a substantially excessive hourly rate. And before you start squawking, let me finish; 2. Recognize that several members of the board, as well as several retired executives, have a serious interest in this case. They were either involved in our initial exploration program in Iran or from companies that also have lost investments in Iran as a result of the Revolution or they spent some time, early in their careers with the state Department or worked in law firms that derive their existence from US State Department business. And 3, the US government has an unofficial seat at the table as to how this case is handled. Our Washington lobbying office receives regular inquiries from the US State Department and other agencies that leave no footprints when they call. I will deal with all that. Just keep it in mind Jack as you proceed." Jack thought a moment and said: "Look, it will take me a great deal of time to get up to speed despite my early involvement in this whole matter. I will work as diligently as I can. I can live with any law firm we use, as long as they aren't doing anything illegal or improper. Cases this big, we should expect big fees, as long as they follow the terms of the engagement. But I want your assurance that if I am responsible for this case, I am in charge, not the law firm, OK?" Jason offered no response over the phone. Jack continued, "If the Board or executives need any briefings on this case, I can prepare you or present updates, written or oral as necessary. The law firm will not, if I am in charge, be briefing the Board. I am not sure that I entirely understand the implications of "board interest" or "retired executive interest", much less the government having a seat at the table. I commit to keeping you in the loop and trust you will help navigate us through the special interests in the case." Jack stopped. Jason responded: "That's what I expect. Just keep me up to speed." Jack thought, I hope this is not the mess that I think it will be. Jason, before he hung up, added, "by the way, Tunesia is your baby too." Jack thought that he better get up to speed on that right away!

CHAPTER 8 — GETTING UP TO SPEED

Now, the storage boxes containing the Iranian files are 12x15 inches and each can contain about a thousand pages depending on how it is packed. Moreover, if the files contain computer discs and the amount of information in these boxes is impossible to calculate without delving into each box. At his first glance at the enormous stack of boxes, Jack had already identified his immediate needs: a seasoned attorney, a team of paralegals a computer wiz and a great secretary. But of course, Jack knew, he would never get approval for additions to staff. But maybe he could see if he could work something out. He called a meeting with three people he had on his staff, his secretary Ella, his paralegal Terry Landy, and a seasoned attorney, his fellow newby and his friend, Steve Baron. Steve had rejected a severance package and requested a reduction in grade in order to stay with the Company. Steve was a great resource as he knew the company as well as Jack did, and more importantly, he knew how to get things done with limited resources. He thought he needed another resource from the financial organization with strong computer skills. He instantly thought of Bert Williams, a crackerjack with financials and systems and the ability to cut through the bullshit hiding the real story. He could make computer programs sit up and bark.

Jack scheduled a meeting over lunch th same day he heard from Jason and, over sandwiches from Primo and drinks, he asked that they volunteer to be part of this special team. Of course, it would be in addition to any other work that they were doing, might involve some travel and of course there could be some risks, a word he recalls mentioning without elaboration. Of course, the work was confidential. If you are asked what you are working on, Jack said,

"Just say you are working on a project for me and that you can't talk about it. If you need information to do your job, just ask for it without any explanation. But almost everything you need will be somewhere in these boxes." He stressed the importance of the project and that it had been around for years without any real progress. Jack explained, it was their job to get the project completed. Without exception, his team said they were in and would work around any other assignments they had on their plate. With that established, he closed the door and began the story of two similar cases: one involving Tunesia, the other involving Iran.

In both cases oil exploration agreements were cancelled by governments and American personnel were expelled from the country. Claims for compensation were made and rejected. There the cases took a different track. Jack began with an overview of Tunesia as he understood it at that point.

TUNESIA

"Here is a thumbnail view of the Tunisian case: Relationships between the countries had been pretty good over the years and contracts for the most part were commercially honored. Disputes came and went but for the most part were resolved by private arbitration under international rules. Tribunals were generally composed of three arbitrators: one selected by one of the disputing parties; the second by the other; and, the third member of the arbitration panel, if the parties could not mutually agree on a person, would be selected by agreement of the two selected arbitrators. Generally, the third arbitrator became the Presiding Judge. Lists of potential candidates were circulated among the parties and procedures were in place to assure that arbitrators with clearly objectionable views could be challenged and excluded. Through this process, a panel was deemed acceptable and after 5 years, hearings were set to be held in Paris, France. I have arranged a meeting with the Company's local French litigation counsel and the arbitrator that had been designated by the Company. I intend to fly out tonight to Paris and report back early next week on the status. All the documents have been submitted and the claim has been teed up and there are no offsetting claims that could be presented by Tunisia. The case, it seems to me, hinges on the question of whether the exploration agreement really was terminated and whether the agreement, if not terminated could have been fulfilled by using third party contractors or employees hired from non-American countries. The arguments Tunisia has advanced were twofold: first, the Company had abandoned the exploration project when riots broke out in the Capital of Tunesia and no expropriation order had been issued by the Tunisian Government; and second, even if there was a fear for the safety of American workers, there was an abundance of available oil field workers from other countries so the work could have been contracted out. Yet, we argue, the Company had plenty of US government communiques to the contrary regarding safety and confiscation. At first blush, the Tunisian Case and the Iranian Case seemed similar, but Jack pointed out, Iran was a different animal. He noted that the documents in the boxes would show that."

Jack concluded his discussion of the Tunisian Case and asked if any questions came to mind. Bert had one. He asked: "You seem to downplay the claim for confiscation and the value of the potential for future oil. Is there something lacking in the case that calls it into question?" Jack paused a bit and resumed his presentation. "We had a partner in Tunesia. They collected all the seismic data, made the calculations and developed the baseline data for the claim for loss of future production. Where that data is located is in question. It is missing and if it cannot be presented effectively, we might as well be presenting a shadow puppet show with a flashlight. We have to be able to present a case, supported with hard data, that we lost the real potential of future loss. Fancy graphs and spreadsheets, unsupported by geophysical data is not very meaningful. Moreover, how we reported this case externally is not helpful. As you know well, Bert, our financial organization never treated the Tunisian fields as meeting the test for booking the assets. Nothing in our own public reports indicates we were adversely affected. How this would play out in the arbitration case remains to be seen. Our financials do support the claim in the Iranian Case. But if we cannot prevail in the Tunisian case, we need to understand how we can differentiate it with the Iranian matter. Perhaps the financials will help is with Iran. We need to construct the arguments necessary to prevail. I will know more after my trip. Then we can really understand the Iranian case. Let me shift to Iran for a few ticks."

IRAN

Jack focused on Iran, "The claim had a lot of starts and stops. Under the exploration contracts, which were negotiated well before the end of the Shah's regime, any disputes that occurred were to be resolved through arbitration. Neither side trusted the courts of the other country of origin and commercial disputes had historically been resolved by international arbitration. Just as the Tunisian contracts had such provisions, so did the Iranian. But this contract called for disputes to be handled in accord with the International Rules administered in the Hague in the Netherlands rather than by arbitrators the parties would pick. Under the Iranian contract, the arbitrators would come from an International group of judges and be selected by the President of the International Tribune. The panel selected was an experienced one and neither party had any disagreement with the three-person panel in place. The real reason for the delay was the entire issue of enforcement. Even if the Company obtained a favorable award from the tribunal, permission from the US Government was necessary. This was true whether the decision resulted in a compromise of claim, payment to Iran or payment from frozen funds to the Company. The US Government was not inclined to provide approval of any matter that could be considered providing Iran a benefit. Enforcement in non-US countries was in question as well. Similar rules in countries aligned with the US made enforcement impossible. Of course, if the parties concluded that there were no funds or properties to change hands, there would be nothing in reality to enforce. But neither party was of the view that the final result would be a zero-sum gain. Both believed in victory and nothing had changed that view. The claims of both sides had been presented to the arbitration panel but, unlike the Tunisian arbitration panel, the parties had limited access to the arbitrators. With the Tunisian case, the parties could talk with their designated arbitrator and see how the panel as a whole was understanding the arguments and evidence. That was not the case with the Iranian claims where the parties were dependent on reading the opposing counsel, who were trained to lie to the other side. It was as reliable as looking into a crystal ball. The Companies could study the pleadings and see the other side's legal position. How deeply the opposite party believed in the strength of their own case, the other party simply did not know. Those pleadings had basically been that Iran confiscated the exploration properties and these properties held enormous amounts of oil and were enormously valuable now and into the foreseeable future. Iran made counterclaims for the nonpayment of the crude cargo that was in the Yabucoa that Jack had sailed away from Kharg Island a decade ago. While there had been many delays in processing the claims and counterclaims and presenting evidence in support of them, the real problem was the US sanctions. The effect of them made direct and indirect payments between the parties impossible and illegal. Even if a settlement of various claims were fair and commercially appropriate, the stalemate between the US and Iran relations made it virtually impossible to make physical payments between parties. A thaw in the process was necessary. But many factions were making that thaw improbable, if not impossible. The hatred existing between the countries ran deep and might not be resolved in our grandchildren's lifetime. It seems clear that the US Government's hatred for Iran stems from the Embassy takeover and the hostages held for more than a year. The fact that a US Company might actually benefit from a deal with Iran does not seem to be enough to overcome the US position on sanctions." Jack stopped and then resumed, "I see no current path to the end. I do not know how to finish this yet." He paused and then said, "Yet"

CHAPTER 9 — PARIS

That night Jack planned to catch the flight to Paris from the International terminal in Philadelphia. Prior to leaving for home to get his luggage, he had asked Steve Baron if he had his passport handy and if he could get a ticket on the same flight. Steve found his passport in his desk and stopped at the Korvette Store in King of Prussia the way to the airport for a change of underwear. He was sitting in coach on the flight to Paris when Jack boarded the plane and sat next to him for the nearly seven hour flight. Within 2 hours of arriving at Charles De Gaulle Airport, Jack and Baron were sitting in the offices of Bernard d'Estange, Managing Partner of the Paris office of the biggest firm in the world Dewey and Cheatham, LLP. Not only the managing partner of the Paris office, Bernard was the attorney, of record, handling the Tunisian case for STAR. After coffee and a cordial greeting Bernard walked them through the case. It was pretty much as Jack had summarized the day before in Philadelphia. While the case would turn on the quality of testimony and evidence of the existence of producible quantities of oil under the lease as well as the possibility of using contractors other than Company personnel, Bernard said, "the greatest weakness of the case is the Company appointed arbitrator." Jack listened intently. This was unbelievable to him. Jack did not react; he waited as Bernard continued, "as you know the Company designated Mark O'Hara as its designated arbitrator." Jack knew of O'Hara certainly but everyone referred to him as Mark O. He had been put forth as the Company's designated arbitrator and his reputation was very strong, a highly respected diplomat of the first order. Mark O was a former US Presidential candidate, a retired Secretary of State, a frequent guest on radio and TV talk shows, and still at his advanced age, a possible Presidential or Vice Presidential nominee under the right political conditions. What Jack had not known, is that the US State

Department had intervened in the designation process with STAR's CEO, and told him that Mark O had to be selected as STAR'S designated arbitrator if STAR wanted favorable support on some pending legislative action. And so selected, Mark O had a great gig, good pay, free room and board in US Housing near the Paris Embassy (a chateau in an exclusive section overlooking the Seine) limo service about town and dining at the best restaurants in the Paris nightly when his private chef was unavailable to prepare meals at the chateau. All this might be a great investment, Jack thought, if the arbitrator was on your side and could influence the final vote on liability. All this Jack had learned from Andy before the case was transferred to Jack. But Jack felt that Bernard was about to drop a bombshell. But before he did, Steve interjected, "Well, I think that a world renown statesman with Presidential presence would dominate any panel of arbitrators and just by a nod here and there would influence the outcome. Isn't that right? What are we missing? It seems easy to conclude that the State Department were doing us a favor recommending Mark O." Jack's thoughts exactly.

Bernard studied both of them. Bernard was an experienced advocate with a lot of miles on his face. His bushy mustache at times masked some of his facial expressions as the listener was drawn to that feature of his face. Bernard began to speak again, his English spoken with a clipped accent typical of the French aristocracy from which he had descended. He dropped his head a little and said: "Gentlemen, Mark O is a complete disaster. Not only is he lazy but he is completely arrogant and so self-assured that his fellow panelists have concluded that he won't even listen to the facts of the case. He seems to think that his charm is sufficient to carry the day. But above all, he just keeps repeating that 'he is a genius' and he knows more about whatever he is talking about than anyone else. But after briefing him last week, it is clear that he thinks this is a case like Iran, only worse for Tunisia. Despite the facts he stated that he believes that the Tunisian oil fields were gushing with oil and that armed terrorists had captured all the company employees and tortured them before expelling them. We can work him through the facts but that is not the basic problem. Mark O, even after living in Paris off and on over the last 10 years cannot understand even grade school French. This is shocking. It would be laughable except that both of the other arbitrators are fluent in French and German and that the proceedings will be conducted in French. This means Mark O has to have a full time translator, not only during the proceedings but during all the private deliberations between his fellow panelists. So when the Tunisian counsel makes a point, the other two arbitrators indicate their agreement before Mark O can get off the dime to interject or question the Tunisian arguments. The problem is that Mark O thinks he is doing a fabulous job and that the Company is likely to prevail due to his fine work. He even suggested to me in our meeting last week that he hoped the Company would consider awarding him some kind of financial reward or even offer him a board position when the case was over." Jack was devastated. He had just heard that Mark O did not understand the case, did not appreciate the fine line between the role of designated arbitrator for the Company and the independence with which he was expected to serve, but he was now seemingly soliciting kickbacks. The worst fact of all was that the case was a loser in the view of the other two panelists. Jack was looking forward to his introductory meeting with Mark O later that day. After Bernard told him the time of the meeting, he mentioned to Jack that Mark O insists on being always addressed as "Mr. Secretary." Wonderful Jack and Steve thought.

The jet lag you experience traveling from the East Coast of the US to Paris and then jumping into meetings is real and even with a good nap after meeting with Bernard, Steve and Jack were exhausted. Only the shocking news from Bernard had kept them awake during the meeting. A brief nap before the session helped immensely. As they entered the meeting room of the Saint George Hotel near the residence of Mr. Secretary, all attendees greeted one another formally. It had been a while since Jack had seen Mark O in a public setting and it seemed that everything Bernard said about him was not an exaggeration in the least. Jack thought that Mark O was aged beyond his years and that he probably never passed up an alcoholic beverage if he could help himself. What a first impression, Jack thought. Jack got right to the point as was his usual behavior and started to review a few points about the case. But Mark O dismissed him saying: "Look we understand this case as if we were arguing it as your counsel and we are convinced that you got screwed by Tunisia and you will prevail. The Tribunal is prepared to go forward with this case. You are in good hands." Jack noticed immediately that Mark O seemed to favor using the royal "we" when referring to himself. Before replying to Mark O, Jack turned to Bernard and said to him in French loud enough to all to hear, "this guy is everything you have described, I think that you should begin talks with Tunisian counsel to settle this case." Jack knew that, as he began his conversation with Bernard in French, Mark O was clueless as to what he was saying. Both Bernard and Jack smiled at Mark O and asked if he wanted more of the sumptuous buffet set out behind them or perhaps another glass of Mark O's favorite beverage. Of course, Mark O, completely clueless, got up and helped himself to another plate of Fois Grass and a double shot of bourbon. The meeting was brief and Jack, certain that Bernard would follow through on his directive in French, took Steve by the elbow and left the room to Mark O and Bernard. They caught the evening flight to Philadelphia from de Gaulle. No worries about Tunesia.

CHAPTER 10 — THE TRAINING RUN

Back at the newly opened headquarters, Jack found himself in makeshift offices nowhere near the executive floor. He might as well have been in another building. He needed to brief Jason as quickly as he could. He decided to do this briefing alone so as not to highlight that two people had traveled on the Company's dime to "Gay Paree" rather than just Jack. Less visibility is sometimes better than explaining the cost effectiveness of a trip with multiple souls. He had two choices to get to Jason's Office. His first choice was to walk seven flights to the top floor and remember to bring his company access card to get to the Executive Suite. His second was to take the elevator down to the ground floor, probably stopping on every floor, and transfer to an express elevator directly to the Executive Suite, of course using his company access card to get on the elevator at the ground floor and then again to exit the elevator on the executive floor. Now keep in mind that, either way, access to the Executive Suite was by executive approval only. You can't just let the rank and file employee walk into the Executive Suite. Sure, there were frequent security bulletins cautioning about some homeless dude following you into secured areas. But Jack always wondered how closely the executives monitored who actually entered into the Executive Suite. Just a passing thought, as he decided to walk the stairs. It was good for his training.

Jason had an office on the hot side of the building with a poor view of the City. As he stood in Jason's waiting room, he looked out the window and then straight down. He could see the loading dock and the driveway between the buildings that the trash trucks used for building access. Wow, Jack thought, seven floors down he had a better view of the loading dock and the windows were cooler because of the shadows from the surrounding buildings. He could not see the trash dumpsters from his office. The real executives, Jack secretly referred to them as the "Head Knockers," had views of the Delaware and Fairmont Park or even the Company refineries and the airport. The views were a nice benefit. Jason did not have such a view. But his was better than a view of the dumpsters.

Jason saw him coming. He stood to greet Jack as he approached the door to the office. As part of the open design of the Executive Suite area, every office had glass walls, some with curtains or sliding narrow panels that allowed some privacy. But no one except the CEO had a door to the office that closed. With "No Doors," nothing could really be a secret from the CEO on that floor. Stylish "Open Concept" design and credit for Corporate Transparency were all achieved and so was feeding the CEO's paranoia. What a world, Jack thought. Jason spotted him a mile away. Jack wondered if his secretary had called ahead to alert Jack's Executive Secretary, Max. Jack stepped into the office and sat across from Jason.

"Well, the trip to Paris confirmed my worst fears," Jack began. "We have spent $15 Million to date and will, at best get a settlement that covers our sunk cost. Can you give me some background on Secretary O'Hara?" Jason said, "you know all the details on his background but he is pretty well connected with some projects that affected the Company a number of years ago. No one is permitted to discuss those events and we never had this conversation. Got it?" Jack nodded and said, "Well Mark O is a liability and I want you to know that the decision to involve him cost the company at least $115 Million. Rulings of the tribunal bar introduction of the quantity of oil resources beneath the fields as well as the projection of maximum production per year as well as the projections as to the life of the production. The tribunal has further precluded the introduction of the data that projected future exploratory wells in the full acreage of the initial exploratory leases. All this means we have a case of a single well that had not produced oil or gas in produceable quantities at the time of the taking by Tunisia. No matter how beautiful the prom dress we wear to the final hearings, we will get destroyed. And the worst of it is that Mark O is clueless. Oh, by the way, I am certain that Mark O has put out feelers that will get back to the CEO that he expects to be considered for our Board in a year or two, just to avoid any suggestion of improper influence. So, I expect that Bernard will be reporting back to me in a week or two with a legitimate settlement offer which will have non-disclosure undertakings as to the underlying facts of the case as well as the studies that were presented to support our claim. But be prepared to say nice things about Mark O's role despite the diminutive settlement proposal." Jason nodded and said, "anything else?" Jack shook his head and got up to leave. Jason said, as Jack headed for the stairwell door, "And keep me in the loop on Iran."

On the way back to his office, he realized that he had time to get to the Downtown YMCA and get in an hour run, grab a sandwich and wipe the remnants of the meeting with Jason out of his mind. He could do that with his runs. While he never lost awareness of his surroundings, when he went for a run, he just could forget the frustrations of work, the depression, the disappointments and the sense of gloom. He could focus on the euphoria of the run. Minutes would turn to an hour and miles would fly by. He could cover better than 8 miles in an hour if he could get to Fairmont Park before the walkers got out to count their steps or the nannies got out with the strollers pushing the kids in their care. He liked it when the weather was spotty as there were fewer out to brave the elements. Sometimes even a brisk winter day would have the advantage of an extra mile or so. Today, he spotted Doug heading out the door of the Y and caught up to him. Doug was going to do a 5 K run and return to the pool at the Y to get in some cross training. Jack caught up a quarter of a mile into Doug's regular course. Jack's normal pace allowed him to converse as he ran. After talking a bit about each's training, Jack began peppering Doug about the government projects that involved STAR in the recent past and how Mark O might have been involved. Doug nearly stopped in the middle of a busy intersection and shut down the conversation. "Jack, are you sure you need to know all about This?" Doug asked. Jack thought about it and said, "I am not completely sure, but if the government is hovering around the Iranian case, I do want to protect me and my team. If it might be relevant, I guess I need to know." Doug stopped, looked at Jack, shook his head, turned around and headed back to the Y. Not as good a training run as he had hoped, Jack thought. He had trouble finishing his planned run.

It was several weeks later that Doug came over to Jack's small conference room, still full of unopened boxes and tables and desks and shelves filled with files. Doug was ready to talk off the record to his team and Jack was grateful. Jack closed the door to the room after his team was assembled. Jack asked Ella if she would take all calls and keep anyone else from coming into the room and said if there was anything she needed to know about all this Jack would keep her informed.

Despite the comfort of the closed door and his concurrence that Jack's team could handle confidential information, Doug asked them to take a minute and draw closer to him. He spoke in a hushed tone, "It began with oil reserves under Columbia and Venezuela. Massive oil and gas resources were discovered by members of the founding family of STAR while on an ecological tour of the country. They became so excited about what they found that they had leveraged the then small company's future on that information and bought every available oil and gas concession they could. They borrowed and then made additional offering of STAR stock to the public to fund the development of Columbian oil. The immediate rewards were staggering. A new refining operation in one of the US Virgin Islands was contemplated as a strategy to keep profits offshore or at least to minimize taxes. It was configured to run exclusively Columbian crude. While this created even more debt for STAR, the rewards proved worth it. Not only did the Company become a real player in the industry, it gave them a seat at the table with both sides of the political aisle. They were becoming the EF Hutton of the oil industry: when STAR talked (which was not very often) politicians listened. A series of events torpedoed this ship of state. First, Columbia threatened the entire oil industry with expropriation if they did not agree to reduce their ownership interest in the oil fields and when that was met with fierce resistance, Columbia just terminated the leases. Second, some guy named Fidel won the day in Cuba and instead of accepting this and using an olive branch, western companies and the US declared an embargo. The history of

Cuba is still being written. The impact on STAR was that a potential market for their refined products was lost. Third, the Company was approached by parts of the Government that have "names that can not be mentioned", in secret, to commission a vessel that would be capable of raising a Russian submarine from the depths of the Pacific Ocean." Doug stopped and looked around the room and said "That's all you need to know about that. We did what was asked and it solidified our relationships with the Department of State, and the "unnamed" agencies in the US Government. But the impact of all this caused discussions between Company lobbyists and the US government to focus on Iran. Seers of the future predicted that crude from a close ally like Iran which was unlikely to confiscate American Companies property was a good bet. And the Company had already believed that the type of crude Iran could produce was a perfect alternative to the Columbian crude that they were going to lose. Let us say that the US Government saw it as an outstanding way to help a political ally as well as be an important chip in the entire relationship with Iran, militarily and economically. Russia had secretly approached the Iranian National Oil Company with an exploration deal and the US Government felt that the US would be better off with a deal with a reliable US Company involved with Iran." That explained in Jack's mind how STAR had been shoehorned into a consortium with Pacific Oil and Calhoun "Well", Doug concluded, "folks that is about all I can say. I suspect that much of the details of how the Iranian deal came to be are NOT hidden in the boxes of files in this room. The US hands probably are not clean. But I believe neither are the Company's. The answers to those questions may not ever be known based on what is in this room. But one thing seems entirely possible. The more you know about where the bodies are buried, the greater the risk to you. And I am not just talking about your pensions and benefits. This is a can of worms. Just be careful. Oh, Jack, Mark O is dangerous and he may not want his past involvement regarding Iran and STAR to see the light of day. Be on your guard." Doug left the meeting room and the team was silent for a long time before Steve asked the paralegal for the next file to review. The work continued.

CHAPTER 11 — BACK TO WORK

Jack continued to handle the day-to-day tasks of his regular job, as well as these International matters that Jason had thrust on him. But those matters would prove to be like wearing a sports jacket to a meeting with folks in suits and ties. He just stood out differently. His staff did not treat him differently. Nor did his fellow attorneys. But the business folks did. Few pushed back if he raised legal issues with a deal and no one objected if he recommended a settlement of a dispute. Some executives and managers sought to deal with one of his reportables rather than bring matters to his attention. Jack saw it happen but felt that each reportable would benefit by handling more challenging questions without his direct involvement. He trusted them to bring things to him when he was needed. One Monday morning he got a call from David Heim, one of the attorneys on his staff, requesting a meeting. Ella set one up for the afternoon. David brought one of the STAR tanker Captains, Jurgin Carlin, along with him. After pleasantries were exchanged David said, "we have a problem with the US Navy. Our ship the STAR ADVENTURE, which is a medium sized tanker, was damaged in transit from our Caribbean refinery to Philadelphia. The damage was not too severe but we will need to make repairs at our shipyard and will miss a voyage and the repairs will be about $500,000. We have evidence that the damage was caused by a Navy vessel off the North Carolina coast at 5:30 am, a week ago." He turned to Captain Carlin and asked him to continue with the report. Carlin was every bit a seaman. He had come up through the ranks but had a military bearing that said, "don't mess with me." Carlin began, "At approximately 5:30 am on April 20 of this year our vessel was struck from above by an object that came from a Navy vessel. This object hit the forecastle and caused damage to the tune of several hundred dollars. Unfortunately, we could not detect any Navy or other vessel in the vicinity of the ADVENTURE at that time. I reported the event to Company Management and David made direct contact with Navy personnel in Norfolk but to date they have rejected our claim, denying any responsibility, denying that they had any vessels in the area and said we could just take the matter up with our Congressman. The message was just stop harassing us" Jack stopped Carlin and looked at David and asked simply, "Well what is the evidence that the Navy had any involvement anyway. What hit the forecastle and do we have pictures or something?" David gleefully opened his file and pulled a half a dozen 8x10 glossy pictures showing the ADVENTURE's forecastle with a surface to air missile imbedded on the starboard side marked clearly on the body of the missile "US Navy." He said, "fortunately it was not armed and we have no idea what was supposed to be the target. We were lucky that the ADVENTURE did not suffer more damage or even catch fire, given the petroleum products it was transporting. I did not have the pictures when I had had my conversation with Rear Admiral Forrestal in charge of Naval Claims in Norfolk." Jack said, "So the Navy's position was, 'not us' and 'we have no knowledge of any incident.' Lets have some fun, if you have a moment." He asked Ella to get Rear Admiral Forrestal on the line. Jack never had to tell Ella how to do her job. She was always direct and took no back talk and no roadblock was too big to block her from her task to make sure her boss's requests were satisfied. Soon Ella called over the intercom, "Rear Admiral Forrestal is on line one, Jack." Jack picked up the call, introduced himself as Chief of Legal Operations for STAR and said, "This is a follow-up to your conversations with one of the attorneys on my staff, David Heim." At that point Jack put the call on speaker, indicated that David Heim and Captain Carlin were on the call with him, and continued to talk. "I wanted to ask you something about our claim for damages to STAR vessel ADVENTURE of $500,000." Jack paused and continued before Forrestal could speak, "Just where would you like us to send the surface to air missile marked US Navy with the identification number USN 99999-567-999. I can arrange it to be picked up by your sailors at out shipyard in exchange for a check for $500,000 this week if that is acceptable." After a few seconds, Forrestal said, "Would this Friday be soon enough? Jack said, I will ask you to call David to work out the details" and hung up. Carlin, David and Jack laughed their butts off so hard Ella had to bring tissues into the office. Sure enough, STAR got rid of the unarmed missile and deposited the check into the Treasury account of STAR. It was just another day in the job of Chief Counsel. They would talk about this for years.

CHAPTER 12 — BACK TO THE INTERNATIONAL STUFF

Jack's voice mail was flashing when he got in the office a few days later. He found that he had two messages. The first one was from Bernard and it was marked urgent. The second was from STAR's Washington counsel for the Iranian case. He had Ella, always the first in the office, place the call to Bernard. Jack opened the conversation, "Hey Bernard, got your message. What is going on?" Bernard jumped right in, "First I have contacted counsel for the Tunisian government and the Tunisian National Oil Company and they are interested in resolving the matter before the final arbitration hearing. I have no guess as to whether they want to pay or receive but I spent an hour on the phone with them this morning and, I think convincingly laid out our case in an effort to get a favorable proposal. I think a settlement of up to $10 Million in our favor is possible. But, more importantly, I want to alert you to the fact that Mark O is lurking in the background about this. I have heard from my contact in the US Embassy here in Paris that he has made calls back to the States to people inside the government and others. He is absolutely livid that STAR would consider settling this case. He is looking for your scalp. So be aware." Jack thanked him for the information and placed a call to Jason who was not in yet. So he left a brief voice mail summarizing Bernard's information on the possibility of a settlement offer and the problems Mark O was raising.

Jack grabbed a large cup of coffee from the beverage station. It was already brewed. Usually, he was the one of the early birds in the office and took responsibility for brewing the first two pots. Today was an exception. One of his team had beat him to it. He pulled a file from the box in the conference room and returned to his office and closed the door. In the file was a biography of Roger Charles,

Esq. of Dulles, Rogers and Kirkpatrick one of the preeminent white shoe firms in Washington. Jack remembered interviewing with them while in Law School and asking the question during the interview process "So what are the plans for improving the diversity in the firm." The response was typical at the time, remember this was at least a decade ago, "Well", the recruiting partner quickly said, "we are opening offices on the West Coast and adding partners experienced in technology ventures all in our efforts to diversify our geographic focus." Jack was stunned, at the time, by the tone-deaf response. Charles was a Yale graduate who had a long career in the State Department before joining the firm as one of the co-managing partners. He was described in several Bar Association publications as rigid, ruthless and as a fierce advocate for US interest and those of his clients, particularly when the interests were aligned. He was afflicted with patterned balding which he covered by a left part slightly above the left ear and a comb over. It enhanced his appearance in the firm brochure and in the several Bar publications featuring the top management of Dulles Rogers and Kirkpatrick. Jack took his time studying the information in the file including the fact that Charles was also counsel for Pacific Oil Company the company that STAR had partnered with in the exploration and drilling concession in Iran. Pacific had an identical case to STAR before the same arbitration panel in the Hague. It was logical that Roger Charles would be acting as co-counsel for both companies. Typically when a matter involves an oil and gas exploration lease, the operator under the terms of the operating agreement between the owners assumes responsibility for the litigation. Early in the proceedings the operator, Calhoun, had tendered their interest to the lease, without compensation, to the two other owners and walked away. Pacific and STAR had agreed that neither would be in charge but would continue using Roger's firm and would jointly manage the litigation. This made communication with counsel somewhat cumbersome and confidentiality solely between one company and counsel meaningless. So, Jack had to be cautious about what he said and whether anything he planned to say would be in conflict with the Pacific position as he understood it. But both companies had unpaid crude cargoes and had been the original parties to the exploration lease with Iran and its government owned oil company. But after the claim was made and the panel selected, there had been little interaction between the companies except through the offices of the general counsel for both companies and a few meetings organized with the attorneys of Dulles, Rogers and Kirkpatrick. As Andy was no longer associated with the litigation, Jack was expecting contact from Pacific but he had heard nothing. Calling Roger Charles after the spinoff was on his to do list. Roger had beat him to the punch. He asked Ella to get him Roger on the line.

Roger was extremely officious and ponderous on the phone. He seemed to chose his words carefully and cleared his throat dramatically as if to assert his control over the conversation. He seemed to expect the listener to be persuaded by every single word. Roger said, "would you mind if a few of the litigation team sat in on this call? While I do not expect them to say a word, I want them to be aware of what we talk about today as it will help them appreciate the importance of the information we will share." Jack said, "Roger, I was briefed by Andy before the spinoff, and I have looked forward to this call since I assumed responsibility for this litigation. The GC has asked me to assume complete responsibility for STAR in this case. It has a very high profile in STAR. It not only is potentially the highest value case from a recovery standpoint, it is the single most expensive case in the history of STAR, in terms of legal fees and expenses. As I am already getting grief on how much your firm is charging us, which as I understand is five times your normal hourly rate, pardon me if I pump the brakes on adding more attorneys to the call. While I have nothing personally against any of your attorneys that may be added to the call, if they stay, I will make sure that STAR will not pay for any time on this call. There will be a time when we should arrange a larger conference call or a series of meetings between your team and mine. And I look forward to meeting each of your team," Jack continued, "as we have not dealt with one another before I want to clear the air a bit. For the purposes of this case, I am the client. I will deal with the office of General Counsel and senior management. Of course, if we have a conflict of views, I respect your right and obligation to go over me if such an occasion arises. But the powers that be have put me in the hotseat and here we are. Obviously, your firm has a great deal of knowledge about the status of the case and expertise in these type of proceedings and I expect you to weigh in with those skills in mind throughout this case. So Roger, what is on your mind?" Roger said, "just a minute while I clear the others in the room from the call." After a short while Roger began to speak again. "It's just us now, Jack. I respect your organizational position and don't see it being a problem. If it should become one, we will talk it through. What I wanted to bring to your attention is that the US, after extensive lobbying from your Company, Pacific and others in the oil industry seeking recovery on claims against Iran, has modified the rules for the transfer of funds between Iran and US Companies effective the first of the year. With an award by the tribunal, like the one we are before, in favor of an American Company, funds may, upon petition, be paid out of the frozen funds held by US Banking institutions. That means after the tribunal awards STAR a sum certain, upon petition, the US Banks in NY would pay STAR the award amount. The US Government has been persuaded that American claims are greater than the claims that the Iranian Companies have against them. Further they will make sure that funds to Iran are still blocked for the foreseeable future. So Jack, this lets us push ahead. We should hold detailed hearings before the tribunal without delay and seek to wrap things up by the end of the year. We won't be in a position, as we are now, of spending money with no end in "sight." "Roger" Jack said, "that is really a positive development. So, let's put a meeting together, go over the basis of our claim, discuss the strengths and weaknesses of the claim and discuss the strategy of our approach with the tribunal. Would next week work?" Roger responded, "How about May 1? That would be perfect for my team. I think Tom Foguard, house counsel of Pacific, is in town that week and might be available. I suggest our law firm host the meeting in our offices because the computer-generated presentation is stored on large Apple based computers are here. If we have the meeting elsewhere, which we can do, it will require the right transportation company to move the equipment and then we would have to set it up. Not having to move the computers will save time and, above all, cost." That got Jack's attention and they agreed tentatively to a meeting on the 1st of May.

Jack immediately placed a call to Jason and, when the phone flipped over to voicemail, he left a short message bringing Jason up to speed on both the gateway to funds after a decision and a meeting date of May 1. He alerted his team and asked Ella to make reservations for the team on the Washington Metroliner for the 1st of May. He told her he wanted to be there at the crack of dawn so he could meet Tom Foguard for breakfast and go over strategy. In the meantime, he and the team needed to finish their work quickly. She gave Ella Tom Foguard's contact information and asked her to arrange a breakfast meeting with him on May 1.

Jack had arranged to drop his luggage at the Doubletree Inn before his breakfast meeting with Tom Foguard. The first Metroliner from Philadelphia got him to Union Station before 7:00 am giving him ample time. Tom wanted to meet in his hotel, the historic and grand Hay Adams. As he entered the lobby of the Hay, Jack got the distinct feeling that guests might have to mortgage their home to stay a night in this place. Jack was guided to a small room off the main dining room where he found Tom Foguard waiting with a cup of coffee sitting in front of him. Tom stood up and shook Jack's hand. "Welcome to the battle against Iran," said Tom. Jack felt every piece of litigation was a battle of sorts because the shareholders were asking him to protect their interests and he always enjoyed the combat of litigation. But he felt that Tom was talking of something else, something deeper, maybe something more deadly. Tom stood over 6 feet and perhaps two or three inches more. Jack had surmised that Tom had seen action on some college basketball team before he had gone on to Yale for law school. Yale! Interesting factoid that that Ella pulled from Martindale Hubbel before he left for DC. Jack wondered how well Tom knew Roger. Tom, after spending a few minutes talking about his trip from LA and how irritated he was to be up this early, given that his biological clock was still on West Coast Time, paused to allow Jack to introduce himself and get acquainted. Tom made it apparent that not only was he upset about the jet lag, but he was also not happy to treat Jack as a peer in any way. He seemed to be put off by Jack's Villanova pedigree and his parent's military background. The only saving grace was Jack's father's WWII service as an officer. While that had peaked Tom's interest, the upbeat mood was deflated when Jack had explained that his father had risen from an enlisted man to the ranks of an officer from Officer's Candidate School rather than graduating from West Point. Clearly Tom felt himself, literally and figuratively, head and shoulders above Jack. Tom began to talk about how important the case was to the country, while seemingly walking past the financial significance to Pacific or STAR. He said, "We are the first case that is close to any hearing before this arbitration panel. Although, on the surface a dispute like this seems to be about money, it is about our National interest. We must never forget that. We were humiliated by the Iranians by the taking of our Embassy. How we handle ourselves in this case reflects on our Country. In the highest echelons of our government, we are expected to erase the national shame of being tossed out of Iran and handing over the keys to millions of barrels of crude and countless quantities of natural gas that will potentially fuel Iran's economic posture. We must handle this case the right way. At this point if this case continues, no viable company will buy any crude that might be sourced from our old leases. Even without the sanctions, who would buy crude that had the threat of a financial claim against it. Delay is in our favor. We must be strong and ignore the temptations of concession. It is a sign of weakness and we must never appear to be weak. The Iranians are savvy negotiators and any hint at concession or negotiation is a blatant sign of weakness to their decision makers." Jack let Tom get to the end of his obviously prepared speech and said, "Lets order a little breakfast and see what we need to accomplish today with Roger and his team." Jack felt that there were big battles ahead and he did not want to begin them right now. In their conversations over breakfast Tom did reveal that he had interned at the State Department when Roger was there and that he had a very high regard for his leadership and intellect. Jack thought this was going to be tough if the Companies were not of the same point of view. As long as they were linked and fighting alongside each other, both cases were worth more. Separately, they may each be worthless. The acid from the coffee began to eat at the lining in Jack's stomach. Jack realized that as long as he held a cup of coffee between his hands, he was less likely to reach across the table and pop Tom in the face. That would certainly be a great way to start. So he let the coffee eat away.

As the meeting with Roger was not scheduled until after lunch, Tom returned to his room in the Hay and Jack went back to the Doubletree. He called Jason and gave him a brief update and asked whether he should meet with the STAR executive assigned to manage exploration. Jack felt that he should brief him before Pacific's executives began reaching out to their peers, perhaps to influence strategy. Tom had asked him this morning the name of the STAR executive responsible for Iran. Jack had anticipated that question and told him it was Joe Camp but he was in the process of moving from Texas to Philadelphia and was unavailable for a few weeks. This would buy him time until he could brief Joe with a strategy he felt comfortable with. Jason said, "You are on your own until Joe gets into Philly and you bring him up to speed," Jason stated. Jack said, "I hope that Tom Foguard will not be a problem in resolving this case. At this point I have doubts that he will be helpful." Jack hung up, put on his running clothes and went out of the hotel for a run. He found a familiar course that went through the Mall, around the Lincoln Monument, passed the Thomas Jefferson Monument and went out to Haines Point and back. For a late Spring morning, it was pleasant. There were still a few cherry trees with blossoms which moved him a bit. He felt refreshed as he got back to the Doubletree. The desk personnel greeted him upon his return, asking him how his run was. He did not think that the Hay Adams staff would have acknowledged his run the same way if he had been staying there. But the run had done its trick. It had gotten his mind off the urge to pop Tom in the face and to lessen the acidic feeling in his stomach. He even began to work on a strategy, but it would take some help from his staff and maybe more than that. Maybe he could call in a few markers and begin the work after the meeting.

Jack met with Steve, Bert and his paralegal Terry for lunch and Jack brought them up to speed. Jack told them to keep tabs on what Tom says and how he interfaces with Roger. And pay close attention to his body language. Is he in the camp of the State Department; does he seem to be under Roger's spell or will he be objective? He said, "don't be afraid to speak up if there are things you don't understand. Don't feel you need to have my approval to take a position. This is a team and you are an important part of it. Before he left for the meeting at Dulles, Rogers and Kirkpatrick, he called Kate who had just gotten back to the house from her volunteer charity work. He told her that he was about to undertake some difficult meetings and that he wished that she were there with him to calm him down a bit as there was someone he might have to pop in the nose if he got out of line. Kate laughed and said, "I know you think a lot about blowing up and popping someone, but you never will. That is not your style. It is not you." Jack responded, "I hope you are right. You usually are."

CHAPTER 13 — THE BRIEFING

The main offices of the firm of Dulles, Rogers and Kirkpatrick was within walking distance of the newly opened metro station in Foggy Bottom. It was somewhat removed from the Capital Building and other Executive Offices but near to the source of much of their legal work, the Department of State. Jack and his team were escorted by primly dressed secretaries to the 19th floor. There they were shown to a conference room, the size of a tennis court, overlooking the Potomac. It was filled with Macintosh computers, overhead projectors and projection screens and before it stood a young Syrian-American, named Abood Jafarr. Jack could tell that was his name from his employee badge on his sports jacket. Abood warmly greeted everyone and then retreated behind his yet-to-be activated computers. Shortly after introductions were made, Roger entered the room, preplanned of course to secure the participant's full attention. Jack and his team were surprised when the six attorneys and paraprofessionals from Dulles, Rogers and Kirkpatrick as a group stood as Roger entered the room. Jack only got up when Roger came over to him to shake his hand. The first half of the meeting was all Roger as he structured his presentation as if he was addressing the arbitration panel. The basic facts were as outlined by Roger.

Here is our case in a nutshell:

A. The duly constituted government of Iran at the time the exploration contracts were signed controlled the national Iranian Oil Company and thereby approved any and all commercial transactions entered into by IOC. While the Government had a veto power, that was effectively waived when the actual work on the exploration work was started and all consideration for the exploration contract was paid as in accordance with customary procedures.

B. Work began approximately 2 years before the "termination of the exploration agreement" and the investment by the consortium (originally including Calhoun but by that time of the case STAR and Pacific were left as part of the consortium) was significant. Seismic data and drilling results demonstrated clear indications of potential sources of crude and its dimensions can be calculated and valued but no well had been drilled that resulted in any quantities of oil or gas in any producible amounts. The work was sufficient to not only justify retaining the areas surrounding the drillings but also the entire acreage of the exploration contract.

C. The regime fell during the exploration work but the IOC had communicated before the "taking" that the work should continue as the new regime had solid parliamentary support. Before the "taking" every indication was that everything should proceed in accordance with the contract. While there was unrest and bodies were being found in the streets or hanging from cranes, the companies were told that they should not worry about any of this. The companies had the full support of IOC until they didn't.

D. The Allatolah had returned from Paris and the uncertainties began. The State Department's view was that the Iranian government had so changed that any assurances from IOC were suspect in light of questions as to the legitimacy of elections to the parliament and appointments to the positions of authority of the officials of IOC. Jack noted this statement but felt that this State Department opinion was not actually shared with anyone in the industry, much less officials of STAR or Pacific. Roger continued:

E. The students invaded the US Embassy, overwhelming the security and took over 300 hostages and the student protests spread throughout the country extending to the oil fields. Roger stopped at that point and noted, "the research of our lawyers indicates that Jack, you were there as a witness to the student takeover at the oil fields and could so testify, right?" Jack said, "Yes, I was there and certainly am willing to testify as to what I recall happened." He stopped well short of what Roger expected his to say. Roger seemed taken aback by his response but continued.

F. So the fields are under the control of elements of the government sanctioned hooligans. Workers are expelled and the contracts are terminated by governmental action or by actions the government did nothing to stop or rescind. The contracts, we have argued, are effectively terminated and work ceased, leaving Iran and the IOC de facto owners of the exploratory property.

G. The papers from the exploration offices prove that the potential of the field was enormous.

At that point Roger introduced Abood to the group and asked him to present visually how the law firm intended to present the data. Abood, with a few keystrokes presented charts and numbers and interpretation of the reservoirs lying beneath the leases. Jack, after hearing Abood show graphically what the data supported, was on board with the following conclusions that Roger summarized:

a. Even showing a high case, a medium case and a low case, the potential for enormous volumes of crude being produced from the existing exploratory wells not completed at the time of the "taking", were in the hundreds of millions of dollars, perhaps in excess of several billion.

b. Depending on the projections of future pricing of crude, even the low case was enormous.

c. If the arbitrators would accept projections of future wells and discoveries as well as assumptions of the number of years such well would produce, the case as presented could support a claim of 5 Trillion dollars.

Jack thought that Roger was going to do a pirouette after he was finished. He had heard these arguments before as Bert Williams had run through them testing the assumptions and projections. The arguments had been considered in the Tunisian case and two of the three arbitrators there had laughed at the testimony. Here the presentation was slick and highly visual. The difference was that the evidence was actually in STAR's hands whereas it was missing in the Tunisian claim. Maybe that could make a difference but the documented evidence would never take a case like this from a multimillion dollar claim to a trillion dollar claim. It would not matter who the attorney was and no matter whether the advocate truly believed the story. He kept wondering whether there was some hidden agenda behind this approach and the size of the potential claim which was staggering. He noted that the Iranian projections were similar to those in the Tunisian case, except for the pizzaz of the graphic presentation. Maybe a deeper look behind the data is warranted. He and Bert would have to huddle.

It was approaching 5:00 pm when Roger had finished his mock arbitration presentation and suggested an adjournment for the day. He walked out of the room to the steady clapping of the Dulles attorneys and paraprofessionals. Jack subtly shook his head. Out of the corner of his eye he spotted Tom joining in on the clapping although he was not as enthusiastic as the Dulles staff.

Over dinner at the Doubletree, Jack made some observations about his meeting with Tom Foguard and the meeting they all had attended. Everyone was impressed with the presentation and how it was presented by Abood. Jack then mentioned an observation, "no one in the meeting today, except Abood, was Iranian or from the Middle East." Terri Land, his paralegal asked, "what is your point? None of us are Iranians either. Don't we have to trust the firm and the opinions of the State Department on the attitudes of the Iranians?" Jack said, "well, I certainly trust that they believe what they are telling us but it is important to get as many viewpoints as possible to avoid tunnel vision." Steve Barron then said, "I have a former classmate that is teaching at George Washington University and I recall him saying there are a few professors on the faculty of International Relations that have an Iranian or Middle Eastern background. Maybe we can find someone with the right background to confirm Roger's views or give us a different perspective. Want to walk over to GW in the morning and scout it out, after your run of course?" Jack thought that was a splendid idea. "Let's meet at 9 and walk over to GW."

CHAPTER 14 — THE IRANIAN

GW has a reputation for educating students interested in international affairs. The location of the University makes it an ideal venue for State Department officials to give lectures and find aspiring students lured by the opportunity of positions with the US Diplomatic service. It was a magnet for internationals, that had experience with foreign governments, to come and either guest lecture or join the diverse faculty. Baron found his former classmate in the coffee shop, the Colonial Caffe. The international students hated the name of the Caffe which was derived from the nickname for the college, Colonial. It reinforced to third world students the entire "colonialist" period. For now it was the Colonial Caffe and Jack and Steve sat with Fred Feldman, Steve's friend. Jack asked if there was anyone on the faculty that could give unbiased input on Iran. Fred instantly mentioned Professor Askari Husseini. He said, "But if you are looking for a bombastic guy or a breast beater, he may not be what you are looking for. On the other hand, you will find him thoughtful, spiritual and deeply knowledgeable about Iran. He is connected with voices on all sides of the spectrum in Iran. While a spiritual man, he is not a mullah or anything like that but he has studied the Quran extensively. His lectures at GW and some of his papers have a ring of a sermon but are tremendously well received. His family was initially associated with the Shah's regime when he was a child but the entire family fled to the US about the time that the US intervened to prop up the Shah. He is fluent in English and several other languages and of course is conversant in several dialects spoken in Iran. Through relatives still in Iran, he retains access to officials in Iran today. Of course the US has conducted deep vetting of Askari and have cleared him and even used him to consult on Iranian/US subjects. He is viewed with great respect, so much so, he is frequently referred to as the 'Iranian Whisperer.'"

Jack reacted to this reference and said: "but is he so connected with the US Government that he cannot be objective in his assessments?" Fred responded: "obviously it is a fine line to walk, a person having access to the US Government and officials in Iran. He understands the risks that exist in that world and the danger to himself and his family in the US and Iran. But he is a man of integrity." Jack was intrigued. "Can you get us into meet with him? I think we should spend a little time with him if he is available."

A meeting was set up for later that morning, but off campus, and nowhere near the Dulles law firm or the State Department offices. It was a small French Restaurant in Georgetown. Jack came alone and saw a small swarthy guy dressed in a blue suit and a white shirt buttoned up to the top but with no tie sitting alone drinking a demitasse sized cup of coffee. Askari rose when Jack entered the small room off the main dining room. Askari shook Jack's hand with a gentle but confident grip. Although Jack was not a towering figure, he stood tall next to Askari. "Let us get to know one another before we talk of business", Jack said. Askari frequently punctuated his sentences with the expression, "blessings be upon you" and "God Willing". For him these were not just a figure of speech. These expressions were sincere and obviously part of his essence. Askari had gentle features, a full nose, black hair kept short, full eyebrows and a striking black mustache that dominated his features. As Fred Feldman advertised, Askari had a voice that almost whispered and not because he was concerned about someone eavesdropping on his conversation. He was low key in every way. He indicated that his father had served in the Armed forces in Iran under the Shah and had interacted with the British, French and American forces that, over the years, had supported the Shah's regime. When his father felt it was time to leave Iran, he found a home in the US as a consultant and advisor to the US military. As his father was a heavy smoker, he was dead before Askari had reached 30. But his father and mother's family contacts had been preserved through the end of the Shah's regime and into the current leadership of the Allatolah. He did not speak of who his contacts were, perhaps for fear that they may be compromised by public knowledge of his relationship or for fear that someone might bypass Askari and contact them directly. Jack spent some time bringing Askari generally up to date on his case, all of which was a matter of public record. He did not intend to share any confidential information. Askari had known of the case. He knew of all the claims against Iran. The STAR and Pacific case was a well-known matter in the Iranian circles in the US and definitely a topic of conversation during his last trip to Teheran. Jack showed his surprise at this. Askari reacted to Jack's surprise. "Why do you act so surprised, Jack. A case in which a company seeks to take trillions if not billions from the Iranian people and fails to pay for crude taken over a decade ago would seem to me to be a big deal for any person in Iran. It is no secret that the Iranian economy is not what it could be. This is the type of thing that political parties and politicians trot out and wave about in protests against the US as well as the Iranian government. This is the type of matter that causes political leaders to lose their heads at worst and their positions at the best." He smiled as he quietly made his points, his eyes staring intently at Jack's face to discern a reaction. After a pause, Askari asked, "How can I help?" Jack began to probe and seek what he was looking for and how Askari might help and how much it would cost. Jack said, "I am being urged by our outside counsel to take this case to a decision by the tribunal. That would be for me the least risky path to take. It might take years before a final decision is made and then unless Iran agrees with the judgment, we will have forever burned our future relations with Iran and other countries sympathetic to their side of the matter. And besides, even with a favorable outcome, the law firm's managing partners will make so much in legal fees that they will be able to establish trust funds so huge their great grandchildren will be giving endowments to their favorite colleges. I get the distinct feeling that my own government, despite the recent decision to allow a path for the payment of resolved commercial grievances is not anxious to see a commercial resolution of this dispute. I may have to demonstrate that we would lose at the tribunal before a commercial resolution would be acceptable to my government. Moreover, I feel that my time at STAR would be very short indeed and there would be even a greater risk for the team working with me." Askari patiently allowed Jack to make his point and said. "Jack, keep in mind that although I was born in Iran, I am an American. I understand the points you are making but we are both Americans." He said this calmly and with no rancor. He had not raised his voice or shown any anger. It was at that point that Jack realized the true measure of the man. Jack just nodded.

"You can help", Jack said, "not by providing legal expertise or sitting as second chair in a mega lawsuit because I have enough lawyers to create a mega firm. I need your measured input, your thoughts on how we could bring this thing to a commercial resolution. What I need is an objective take on how the Iranian decision makers might think; how they can be influenced and how what I say or propose would be received and understood. For example, it is standard State Department doctrine that 'Iranians only respect strength and that any proposal that seeks to find middle ground is a sign of weakness and perhaps even a signal of surrender. I think that bias stands in the way of resolving the dispute. Each side could be sitting for years waiting for the other to suggest a resolution. Any thoughts on that?" Askari did not blink. In fact, his eyes had never moved from staring at Jack as he explained his position. Again, Jack felt as if Askari's whole brain was focused on his answer.

Askari began, "of course proposals weakly made or poorly presented by parties that are unknown to an opposing party can be perceived as a weak one. I would agree with that. And experienced negotiators know when one side or another is in a weak position. That is not a cultural or national thing. It is based upon the skills of the party to the negotiation and their experiences. Such a suggestion that compromises per se are a signal of surrender or a sign of weakness seems more like an argument by a classic plaintiff's lawyer than the views of a seasoned diplomat. It is plainly wrong and calculated to make you fearful of attempting to settle, if I may say. But in the dynamics of a ten-year gap between two opposing sides, knowledge of what each side means when it uses words or presents proposals makes sitting across the table from one another a challenge. Much like a card game, whether it is poker or a game of fish, if you know the cards your competitor holds it may matter little what attitudes the other side has. What may matter more is whether your moves are more like chess. An experienced chess player understands the moves an opponent makes and their short- and long-term intentions as well. Of course, an expert can disguise what a move might mean. Experienced chess players do. You just need to watch and respond with care. If you understand what motivates the IOC and their representatives, you are playing a game of multidimensional chess. If you would like me to give you that advantage, I suggest the following arrangement: I play a role consulting with you and your team. My involvement would be above board and visible. I would not serve as an advocate in meetings but be supportive and helpful as appropriate. I would assist you in making proposals of your choosing and be available to advise how, when and where to communicate them. I am willing to travel to Iran to support and advocate for any proposal when it is in my opinion ripe and timely. I will be candid about the possibility of success of any of your proposals. I would seek to learn of Iranian counters to your proposals and provide you with my thoughts on when or how to respond. If I am successful, I should expect a success fee. I leave the amount to your judgment. If nothing is generated, you would owe me nothing except my expenses. I place my trust in you that if in your opinion I am not adding value, you can terminate the arrangement, owing only my expenses. I believe you are an honorable man and if that is agreeable, I am willing to be your Iranian Consultant."

Jack said, "one more thing that I would like to add. Pacific is in this with us and I would like them to enter into the same arrangement, thereby doubling the fee and sharing the expenses. If that is acceptable, we have a deal." Jack gave him a moment to consider and stretched out his hand. The two shook hands over the arrangement. Jack felt that this was the best contract he had been party to since law school.

Jack had the time to check his messages and found one from Jason. Jason had left a voice mail that Joe Camp was ready to talk about the case and provided Jack with Joe's new executive Secretary's number. Jack called him and for the next hour he outlined the case and reviewed the strengths and weaknesses of it and the possibility of getting Pacific and STAR to jointly engage Askari as a consultant that could get this whole case resolved. The goal would be to get it done in the fourth quarter for financial reporting purposes. He told him he had a handshake deal with Askari which he planned to review with Tom Foguard soon after his call with Joe. Joe told Jack that he agreed that a quick resolution was highly desirable particularly if STAR could only get a "fraction of a fraction" of the claim that Roger was planning on presenting to the tribunal. "How can I help" asked Joe. "You have the reigns and have my complete confidence. Coming down and talking with the lawyers seems a waste of my time and I would just be a squeaky wheel." "Well," Jack said, "you could get on the phone and talk with your counterpart at Pacific and lean on him or her a bit about settling this bear under the right circumstances and for the right financial terms, even if it means giving the State Department a stiff arm to get over the finish line. That is our objective as I see it, get this thing resolved, stop the bleeding in legal fees and expenses and put us in a better commercial position if STAR or its successor wants to have any relationship with IOC or its successors or even others in the international community selling crude or natural gas." Joe agreed to make the call that evening. Jack had his Iranian consultant and maybe this could be brought to an end.

CHAPTER 15 — SHIFTING THE POSITION

Back to the offices of Dulles, Rogers and Kirkpatrick, Jack took Abood aside and began to talk with him before the meeting began and his fellow lawyers and paraprofessionals arrived. Jack wanted to find out more about this impish attorney with superior computer skills and an encyclopedic grasp of the facts of the case and the legal position. Jack had closely observed him throughout Roger's entire presentation. He was mouthing every word that Roger was saying and giving hints to him whenever Roger seemed to hesitate or go off the reservation. Clearly, Abood had written the script in addition to being the architect of the visual graphics and in all probability with developing the entire financial projections supporting the claim that the firm was working to present to the arbitration panel. Jack thought, this guy was indispensable. Was he a good hand? Would he be capable of taking the lead if asked. Had he consumed the State Department Kool Aid. Could he just represent his client to the best of his ability. The discussion brought Jack closer to his answers.

The attendees were gathered when Roger again, as yesterday's meeting began, made his grand entrance. He seemed to expect a pep rally to breakout. But instead, both Tom and Jack, now sitting close together turned to Roger and nodded his entrance at the same time. Jack thought, something must have happened since yesterday. Maybe Joe happened. He could be a real bull when pointed in the right direction. As Roger entered the room he had paused and noted that Jack and Tom were at least aligned in their physical position, he paused and waited for the message that he sensed was coming. He was no novice. He could read the room.

Jack remained seated but looked around the room and began to talk, loudly and forcefully. "Thanks for the presentation yesterday, Roger, and to your entire team for putting all the work into a strong and terrific overview of our case. I am speaking now for STAR, as I leave Pacific to provide their own observations. The data and arguments make this a case so huge that I feel that the Iranians and the IOC will fully understand the risks of going to a full hearing on this case. So presenting this case or even the damage projections will probably cause the Iranians to react as they have reacted since the claims were filed. They will delay. And they will delay till the cows come home. I would. You would. And STAR and Pacific will continue paying legal fees and the case will not go away. The projections, I am sure have been shown to the Iranians through the normal course of discovery. I feel that, as impressive as they are presented, the projections will not cause the Iranian's knees to wobble and bring them to the negotiation table. They will just ignore them no matter how convincingly the computer programs demonstrate how much they could pay. I feel at the end of the day, neither company will ever receive a dime from Iran during what is left of my career with STAR if we present this in the context of a demand. I have seen these types of projections and the reaction an arbitration panel, composed in part of arbitrators we had a hand in forming, laugh at the numbers and the projections. I do not anticipate a different response.

Even if we are ultimately to see money from this dispute, by way of negotiation, it is inconceivable that any settlement will result in payment along the lines of the high, medium or even the low case projections. I firmly believe that representatives from Iran are not only experienced diplomatic negotiators, they are also savvy international commercial negotiators. Having said that, I feel very strongly that STAR has the right team from a diplomatic point of view and international commercial point of view to bring this case to a swift negotiated solution and obtain payment out of the frozen accounts by year end. We just need to have realistic expectations." Before Roger could speak, Tom weighed in. Jack had no idea what he would say. But he had hope. Tom began, "Jack, while I am not sure that I completely agree with everything you said, I want everyone to know Pacific is in favor of somehow ending this process with a settlement, a reasonable settlement, and if possible, by the end of the year. Pacific wants to end the bleeding from the legal and other costs of this case."

Roger stared at Jack and Tom for what seemed to be hours but probably was the span of a minute before he spoke. "Gentlemen, I am sure that when you check back at your home offices you will find that you both are off the reservation. The other side in this war, and I use that term seriously, would eat you up the moment you suggested a negotiated solution. Based on the collective experience of our firm, you would be making a serious blunder even to hint in any way that you are not going through to the presentation of this case to the tribunal. You would be better advised to sit there while I make our forceful case to the tribunal and wait for a decision. You have heard our arguments and presentation of the facts. How can you honestly question a successful outcome. Besides I do not believe that the State Department would be very interested in seeing a negotiated outcome." Jack responded: "We can discuss at length the wisdom of your "war strategy" versus one that I am suggesting which is to pursue a high-level negotiation under the right circumstances coupled with conveying the companie's willingness to pursue a "war strategy" if there is no evidence of a serious negotiation by the Iranians. But I am troubled by your suggestion that the State Department or any other governmental agency would not be interested in seeing a US company improve its bottom line significantly and in the near term. Is there some problem of which you are aware? Is there something we need to know?" Roger just shut down and seemed to back off whatever he wanted to say. Jack seemed to feel maybe he was getting too close to something. "It is my opinion and that of this Firm" Roger said, "that the Iranians do not fully appreciate the strength of our case and the risk to them of the size of the award that could issued by the tribunal. After they see our evidence and our case, I feel they will change their opinion. I agree that they do not at this point appreciate how bad it could be unless their own lawyers have done a downside analysis of the evidence exchanged to date. Knowing the caliber of their attorneys, how many times the Iranians have changed their trial counsel, and seeing the house counsel for the IOC, I feel that no one on the Iranian side is thinking about the risk of a huge adverse decision." Jack observed, "It seems to me that your job, following this meeting, is to somehow impress upon the Iranians the risk they are facing. Take a few days and work on an approach and get back to us. And if there is something lurking within the bowels of our government that might disrupt a commercial resolution, I expect you to let me know." Jack stared at Roger and then got up and left the room.

The trip back to Philadelphia was a quiet one. No one on the team seemed to have anything to say. Jack took the time to visualize his scheduled long bike ride to Reading, Pennsylvania, a small town about 50 miles away from his home outside of Philadelphia. The plan was for Jack and Doug to ride to Reading and back that Saturday. It would be a good way to put the developments in the case in perspective as he rode and to think about anything but the case as the miles went by.

At the break of day Saturday, Doug rode his bike to Jack's home and waited for Jack to emerge from his garage. They checked with each other to see if each was ready to do this, lights, fluids, bike tools and other pitstop necessities. Kate had asked if she could accompany them by car as she thought a visit to the outlet shops in the Reading Flea Market and lunch with the guys seemed like a great outing. She had frequently ridden her own bike accompanying Jack on a few long rides, but she felt that she would slow him down at this point of his training. Rendezvousing in Reading seemed a good compromise. It was about 50 miles each way and Jack was interested in miles at this stage of his training as much as speed or feet of climbing. His wife would start out a few hours later than Jack and Doug. Doing a ride of this distance would give Jack a time to relieve the tension and anxiety of the past week. Doug and he could talk from time to time where the shoulder of the road was wide enough and the traffic was light. Weekend traffic was usually light early in the day. To commemorate their training, Jack had talked the local Trek store in Wayne to print up bike shirts that said "Training for Tri" on the back and "Finish the Race" on the front. Jack thought the jersey was really cool and gave one to Doug before the ride. Anything to keep the juices flowing was helpful.

It was about 11 am and they were in the home stretch to Reading on a wide open stretch of Route 322 which was about the safest point of the outward-bound leg of the trip. Both Doug and Jack always rode with mirrors secured to either their helmets or their sunglasses. As one aged, relying on the sounds of traffic to the rear and the loss of neck flexibility necessary to turn and see traffic was difficult. Doug was in the lead about a bike length ahead. In his mirror, Jack, could see two black vans proceeding rapidly in the same direction Jack and Doug were traveling. Jack remembers calling out to Doug, "car back" as the first van hit Jack's bike with a glancing blow which caused him to touch wheels with Doug's bike jerking Doug's bike to the ground and under the wheels of the second van. Jack never saw Doug fall as he was down and lying on the shoulder of the road in excruciating pain. Doug lay breathless beneath his bike. Both vans sped off but not before Jack's brain caught an image of the rear of the vehicles. It was about this time that Kate, running slightly ahead of her predicted arrival time in Reading was slowed by a long line of vehicles and the flashing lights of emergency vehicles. Slowing. she saw the cause of the delay: two ambulances, two other rescue vehicles and several State Troopers slowing down traffic. She immediately saw Jack's messed up Trek and another bike she felt must be Doug's and pulled over to the annoyance of the State Troopers. She jumped out of the car and proceeded to cry out, "I know them. One is my husband Jack and the other is his friend Doug. They were headed to Reading. How are they? What can you tell me? Where are they taking them? I have to go and be with Jack and his friend." She was beside herself. Not waiting for responses to her questions, she pulled out and followed the two ambulances to Reading Memorial Hospital which was about 15 minutes from the crash scene. As she drove off, she could see in her rear mirror that the bikes were beyond salvage. She followed the ambulances to emergency entrance to the emergency entrance to RMH and went in. Unless you are from another planet, you know how a wife under all those conditions will just take control. Both riders had carried ID, a little money and a credit card and their phones. Fortunately, the emergency feature on their phones allowed emergency personnel to access insurance information as well as their drivers license information. The EMT guys had all that information and had radioed it to RMH emergency personnel. Kate, waiting in the ER area, demanded to know Jack and Doug's condition. She knew that the weekend staff of hospitals in the outlying communities was usually comprised of interns and second-string doctors. The staff told her to wait and the surgeon would meet with her. She was surprised when a fit middle aged doctor came through the doors of the ER ward and went straight to her and spoke: "Are you Jack's wife, Kate? I am Dr. Chidester," reaching out his hand to shake hers. "Your husband is alert and in great pain. He has a probable concussion and a hairline fracture of the femur close to the hip. It did not require a hip replacement or any extensive reconstruction of the femur to heal. I placed his leg in a temporary cast which may well be replaced in about two weeks with a removable one, but otherwise he will make a full recovery. He will be riding in a couple of weeks, if you give him permission. But his companion is another matter. Can you get us in contact with his family. We need to get permissions and input as we proceed with further care." Kate said, "Yes, I have it all here now that I have gotten into Jack's phone. I have given it to the staff here and they should be in contact with his wife, Anna. I have talked with Anna and she is on the way here. It will be at least an hour before she gets here. Here is her cell if you need it before then. Can I see Jack?" Dr. Chidester said, "sure" and showed her to Jack. She was certain that Jack will want to know how Doug was. She had no information for him. Dr. Chidester would not say anything.

CHAPTER 16 — THE FIRST STEP

Jack had breezed through the emergency room, rejecting any pain-relieving medication that might be addictive or have any lingering impact on his ability to make significant decisions. Jason, who had been alerted to the accident by Kate, appeared at the RMH Monday morning. He learned that Doug had been transferred to Penn. He wanted to talk with Jack before he was discharged. Kate was surprised at this as Jason was never very concerned about the health of his staff. Her impression of him was that he was probably more concerned with the insurance chargebacks to his department than the health of one of his attorneys. Well, maybe she could be wrong about that. From the nurse's station she could hear loud voices from Jack's room. Then Jason left and all was quiet. Jack said, "All is good. I just need to be able to take a few steps to the end of the corridor on my walker and then I will earn my certificate of discharge." With the determination of an athlete at the start line of the Boston Marathon, Jack pulled himself to the edge of hospital bed, grabbed the handles of the walker, eased himself to the floor and took the first step. It was as tentative as his first as a baby learning to walk. Dr. Chidester had done a good job casting the leg. The leg would work once it healed; he felt no pain; he might have to be careful about putting his full weight on the leg for a while but he was confident he would be back to running, biking and swimming before Dr Chidister's projected schedule. He had learned from Kate that that was not going to be the case with Doug. He asked Kate to check his things to make sure that the blood soaked bike shirt was in his take-home plastic bag, rode the elevator to the exit with his insurance bought walker, got into his wife's car, closed his eyes and went home.

It was a week later that he limped into the office and greeted the staff who welcomed him back to work. He spent as little time as he could thanking them for their well wishes. Responding to the pointed questions about Doug, he could only say, "he will be home in a week" and "you know, I cannot explain how the van hit us as we were both well inside the shoulder area of the highway." He planned on going to see Doug that morning to talk with him about the accident, which in his opinion was not an accident at all. For now, he had to catch up with things. Ella brought him a stack of pink slips that contained about 25 messages, most of which were from well-wishers. But one was from Abood and he asked Ella to get him on the line after he returned from the Penn Hospital where Doug had spent the last week after transferring from RMH. He would take a ride service to Penn because walking with a temporary cast was not in the cards.

The early diagnosis at RMH was that Doug had his pelvis crushed and that several organs, including his liver and kidneys were severely damaged. Penn was the immediate answer, and he was medevac'd there while Jack was undergoing the procedure to cast his leg. Clearly, riding a bike was not in Doug's near-term future and neither were the plans they had for some bike races they had talked about before the ride to Reading. But he was alive and would recover, eventually. Jack, using his walker, entered Doug's room where there were set up rehab devices, including a device that resembled a bowflex which he could use for arms, his shoulders and abbs. A bike with a ribbon tied into a bow was in the corner of the suite. It was a gift from the law department. While it seemed a cruel hoax, given the time he would spend on his back, Doug thanked Jack and the department for the gift and said that he would use it to motivate him to recover. Jack said, "Just get well. That is all that anyone can expect. You will do what you can going forward." Doug nodded, looked at Jack and then said quietly, "Jack, this was no fricking accident. We were targeted. It was sunny. We were lit up like Christmas trees. We were so close to the far edge of the road we could have picked dandelions. The driver just took off and left us for dead. Who does that? I know that the number of bike accidents is rising each year. But again, this seems to me to have been no accident. And to put a finer point on it, I was interviewed by three members of the State Police when I got out of surgery here at Penn and then nothing…" Doug stopped mid-sentence. Jack asked, "What do you mean nothing?" Doug said, "I mean, I called the barracks near Reading and found that the troopers were reassigned and that there was no investigation on going. The matter was determined officially to be an accident. Nothing was done to identify the driver; the report suggested we may have strayed too close to the traffic lane or that the driver was distracted and unintendedly hit us. It's just 'BS'." When he decided to visit Doug, he had clearly intended to grill him about his recollections about the wreck. Jack could not think of any reason why anyone would intentionally do this to either of them. Of course both were connected with the Iranian case, or at least it was well known in STAR that he was regarded as "Mr. Iran." Doug had a history with the company and had conferred with Jack and his team off the books so to speak. But it is possible that Jack alone had been the target and Doug's injuries were just a consequence of Jack being targeted. A case of wrong place, wrong time. Jack had counted on an official police investigation to give them answers. This was disappointing. Jack, seeing anger and frustration all over Doug's face said forcefully, "You may be right, Doug, we won't let this go until we find out some answers. In the meantime, get well." All Jack could think about as he got into the shuttle back to the office was the sensation of a van striking him and Jack falling to the ground. Like a tune that rattles around in your brain and you can't get out of your mind, the fall would not go away. Was someone trying to stop him? Could that be the reason? Jack was just guessing. But something deeper was rolling around in his mind, the rear of the vehicles. There was something about them he could not clearly capture. It would come to him eventually.

Back in the office, Ella got Abood on the line. When he was connected, Abood said, "Thank you Jack for returning my call. I am glad to hear your voice and understand you are going to recover but that is not the reason why I originally called. Can I call you back from another number in about a half an hour?" He then abruptly hung up. Curious.

Jack returned to his other messages. One had been from Jason and he called him back. "Jason, back in the saddle today. Saw Doug today and he really looked good and appreciated the gift the department gave him. He is not chomping at the bit to get back in the office yet but knowing him, that will come shortly. Wouldn't surprise me if he just shows up some morning, briefcase in hand. Well, should we resume our conversation when you were paying your respects in my recovery room?" Jason said, "I understood your points and I believe that the position you have carved out, namely, negotiate from strength and get this done quickly and stop the bleeding of costs, is sound. Joe Camp agrees and apparently has considerable influence with upper management on what you plan to do. I have gotten no pushback from any of senior management or the CEO. You should know I have received some messages from Mark O wanting to talk about both cases. That seemed puzzling. His messages indicated he knew all about your accident and nothing had made it in the press, other than two cyclists were hit by vehicles. And as to Iran, he does not have any involvement or even knowledge about Iran does he?" Jack answered "Glad you are on board with the strategy and that I am not out on the proverbial limb by myself. To answer your question about the so called 'Mr. Secretary', he is not in any way involved in Iran. But I cannot rule out contacts with him emanating from the State Department, particularly if they were indirectly generated by Roger. I am seeing a tangled, incestuous relationship, and it is not at all good." Jack chose not to raise Doug's concerns then about whether this was really an accident. He could feel Jason nodding through the line as he hung up. If Jason knew anything about the historic relationship between Mark O, STAR and Iran, he chose to keep quiet.

Ella came into his office and said that Abood was on his line and that it did not appear he was calling from the Dulles phone line. Jack took the call. "Jack let me get right to it as to the reason why I called. For reasons that should be apparent to you, I must withdraw from the Dulles firm and, with two of my fellow attorneys from the Dulles firm, offer my legal services to you and your company. I can take virtually nothing, document wise, from the firm. But all the underlying documents are STAR's anyway. All of the computer programs and graphics must stay with the Dulles firm of course. The truth is that all of that data, the projections and even how it should be displayed was the result of Bert William's work product. Reconstructing the graphics and the financial projections are an overnight job and I can have it running on STAR's computers within a week. But my thoughts, my legal skills and advocacy are at your service, now if you please. Whether you accept my offer of legal services or not, I intend to incorporate as The Abood Law Firm, LLP as of today. Our practice will be International Law and Transactions. Let me say that three things have triggered this decision: first, I agree with you completely about negotiating a resolution with Iran; second, the companies, both STAR and Pacific are being hosed as far as legal fees and costs are concerned. I can do the work faster, better and cheaper than Roger and his team can; and, third, I was not part of what happened to you last weekend on Route 322 near Reading Pennsylvania and I want no association with the Dulles firm who, if they were not responsible, would have benefitted from taking you out of the command and control of this case; and their ties to the government makes ruling out government involvement in your accident questionable. Think about it but I will be informing the managing partners in the Dulles firm of my decision. I expect Roger will be immediately on the phone to you, calling to protect the firm's investment." Abood disconnected the call.

Jack was shocked but as Abood was talking, it all made sense to him. It all fit together. The fact that Roger had not contacted his office or him after the accident had been curious. He double checked all his pink slips and found no messages from Roger. He asked Ella if she had received any calls from Roger and she confirmed that there had been none. Surprising that Abood heard about it, but Roger was oblivious. The general news of the accident had been reported in the Lancaster County Times, the Philadelphia Inquirer, the API bulletin as well as the Corporate Counsel Times. It was not a secret. And yet Mark O 'had been aware. Well, this was a development that he needed to talk with Tom Foguard about, and of course Jason, at the right time. The next pink slip had the home number for Bernard on it. It was approaching 10 PM Paris time. He hoped it was not too late.

CHAPTER 17 — THE INTERPLAY BETWEEN CASES

But Jack made the call anyway and Bernard answered on the first ring. Bernard asked Jack how he was and confirmed from Jack what he already knew, he was back in action and ready to roll. Bernard, having dealt with the courteous inquiries wanted to bring him up to date on the Tunisian case and some developments that Jack needed to know. Bernard said: "The Tunisian government is most eager to put this matter behind them and is willing to pay a sizeable amount to do so. I did present your high figure for their consideration and your concerns with keeping all data and proprietary calculations confidential. They are on board with your proposals, agree to your proposed number, which by the way is twice what I had felt we could get, and they have indicated that this will happen this month. I can have the settlement document in your hands and theirs by weekend. We can have a signed deal then by exchanging faxed signature pages and agreeing to exchange formal signature pages over the weekend. Funds would be available, as I said, by the end of the month." Jack asked, "is there anything that the arbitrators could do to disrupt this? Would this be a done deal?" Bernard said "we would notify the administrators of the tribunal in Paris to mark the case as disposed as of the date it is signed and we would then notify the arbitrators that their services were ended as of the same date. We are not required to disclose the terms of the agreement and it would be unusual to do so. We would ask them to present final invoices for services through the effective date to both parties to be split equally." Jack said this was perfectly agreeable and that he would send the wiring instructions to Bernard's office tonight. Bernard said, "Excellent! I did say that the arbitrators had no ability to stop this deal, but you should know Mark O is ranting and raving about his dignity and how he has not been shown the respect his legacy deserves. He kept saying to me on the phone the other day that he knew people in the State Department were watching STAR and that they shared Mark O's views that STAR must be brought back into the fold even if that meant changes within STAR to accomplish that. I did not understand what he meant but I wanted to make you be aware that he is a troublesome guy and maybe dangerous." Jack asked Ella to talk with Bert Williams and get the wiring instructions from STAR's finance department and to advise that a substantial wire would be forthcoming within the week. Once she had the wiring instructions, she was to prepare a communication to send to Bernard's office. It should go out, if possible, by the end of the day. With Ella, he assumed it would done. "Asked and done Ella."

He called Tom Foguard and spent a great deal of time on the conversation, but he knew that he had an extra window of time as Tom, being in LA, had an extra three hours of time. Jack was used to working late. He covered a range of topics, from his recovery to the shocking news from Abood, the potential deal with Askari and the strong possibility of STAR settling its Tunisian arbitration case. He held back the suggestion that Abood had made about the Dulles firm and his "accident" and Mark O flipping out and seeming to make threats. He would pick and choose when he made that known to his new partner. Jack also identified Joe Camp as STAR's executive contact. However, Tom obviously knew of it as his business client Mike Shepard had brought him up to speed about Joe and Mike's conversation. Tom told him Mike was an EVP at Pacific and that Joe Camp and Mike had known each other for many years.

Jack, feeling they were on the same page, signed off for the evening. They had agreed on engaging the new Abood firm as well as jointly hiring Askari. It would be left to Jack to work through the change and tell Askari both companies were on board with his involvement. A lot was accomplished on the first day back.

Day two and no bike, run or swim before the office. Maybe he would throw away the walker and start using a cane once the temporary cast was removed. Jack was missing his normal ways to deal with the stress. Ella was prepared, as usual. As he used his walker to get to his desk, she placed a tall cup of coffee on his desk, near his right hand and put the usual pink slips in the middle of his desk. He thought a few moments before he called Askari and looked at the backpack hanging now on the back of the office door. He asked Ella to hand it to him and he got out the two cylinders. Ella then left his office as he opened them and looked at the same rolled up scrolls he remembered seeing before. Just handwritten letters or symbols in Farsi. Maybe Askari could look at them and see if we can use them in some way. He hit the intercom and asked Ella to take the scrolls, photocopy them and send the copies overnight to Askari's office. Ella asked whether he wanted it sent via the Company courier to the DC office and then hand carried to Askari? The company did still send same day packages to the corporate affairs offices in Washington DC, but he did not want anyone in the STAR DC office to see these papers. Maybe he was paranoid. Jack said it would be too visible that way and Faxing would not be as confidential as just putting it in an overnight delivery envelope. Jack said, "I do not know what these scrolls say and I want to keep this under wraps for now. So just use the overnight delivery service." Then he dialed Askari's number and updated him about a few things.

"First, I want to confirm that both Pacific and STAR are fully on board with our engagement of you as our Iranian consultant. I will ask my finance and computer guy to get with you and go over the projections and forecasts regarding possible production from the exploration leases. His name is Bert Williams and he will come to your offices or wherever is convenient and bring you up to date. Next, I want to tell you that we are separating the litigation into two legal groups. Dulles Rogers and Kirkpatrick for now will began to disengage, or at least back out of the lead position. The lead will be taken up by the Abood firm which is being formed as we speak. It will be at first a small firm comprised of a few of the Dulles lawyers headed by Abood. All of them have cut their teeth on the Iranian case. That group will get us to the finish line. I am going to keep the Dulles firm on the engagement for now as we may need some guidance to get us through the State Department obstacles that may arise. Abood's lawyers may be able to fill this role with time. We will see. As this progresses, I will keep you up to date. Neither firm knows of your engagement and I feel at this point that is as much for your protection as it is a way of keeping the firms focused on the litigation." Askari interrupted, "Why did you say, 'for my protection'." Jack said, "well that was my next point. In my discussions with Abood, it was suggested that my 'accident' near Reading was no accident. He shared no information about who might have done it but that is in part why Abood's group is leaving the Dulles firm. Further, you may know that Mark O, or if you prefer 'Mr. Secretary' has made veiled threats to disrupt any potential resolution with Iran either on some historical or policy grounds or as a possible payback to ending his gravy train with the Tunisian arbitration. I don't know how serious that is but as far as I am concerned, my crash was evidence enough that I may have a target on my back." Jack could hear Askari nod. 'Lastly, I am sending to you copies of two scrolls or documents that were given to me during my escape from Iran a long time ago that contain writing that most probably is Farsi. Take a look and if helpful, feel free to use the content. I have the originals." Askari said, "I will review and use them as appropriate. I had planned to go to meet some of my contacts in a week. But I expect that my travel will be monitored considering the information you have given me. I will figure out another country to meet in. I will contact you when I get back." They disconnected the call. Jack was getting paranoid. Could someone be listening to his calls? He thought a call to the Security department was in order.

Jack took a breath and made his call to Roger. As the phone rang in his ear he still had not decided how he was going to say, "You are fired." He was going to wing it depending on how Roger responded. Roger answered the phone and immediately took over the conversation, "Jack, so good to hear you. I had been meaning to reach out to you after the accident and I heard about your broken leg and before I could get to it, I learned you were back in the office. Remarkable! All that exercise has truly paid off. I trust your colleague will recover." Jack thanked him for his concerns and said that Doug was doing well but his recovery would just take time. But before Jack could get to the points he wanted to cover, Roger jumped back in, "Jack a lot has transpired since you were here in my offices. First, I am aware you want to work with my former junior law partner Abood and I want to make sure that this all goes smoothly. I think that my firm can continue to add real value to this case and I want to work with you to make that happen. We can make the legal services of the two of our legal firms seamless and cost effective. You have my full commitment to do that. I truly believe that a case that has international implications needs the expertise and relations I have with the US Government to bring this case to a successful conclusion. If that is not the case going forward, I will gladly withdraw." Jack stopped him, "Roger, you need to know that I think that you are an arrogant SOB, but I clearly see how the Iranian's litigation counsel would fear you and your firm. I expect that the Iranian government and the IOC are well aware of your reputation and that is a good thing, so far. Your involvement, in my view, serves a purpose. It shows that we believe in the strength of our position and that they are in deep dog dirt if they go to a tribunal hearing. Let's go forward together with this understanding: you are the face of the STAR litigation for now and the Abood firm will do the work to put us in the best possible position whether that is a trial before the tribunal or negotiation. And I want the total costs to go down. OK?" Roger agreed.

Roger then continued, "the second matter I want to discuss with you is that there are rumors that either I, or someone in my firm, had something to do with your accident. I assure you that is not true in any way. I acknowledge I have had discussions with the State Department about the case and the principals at State in charge for Iranian matters. They did ask for projections on timelines and questioned me about strategy. I did update them as to the developing strategy you were advocating. That might have been a mistake. But it should not surprise you that State would want to know how a huge claim against a nation, with which the US is not on the friendliest terms, is progressing. That should not be totally unexpected by you. It certainly is not unprecedented. It happens in all these high profile cases. You should know that the State Department has a deep hatred for Iran. The players are new but the institutional hatred for what happened at the US Embassy in Tehran has not been forgotten and is probably unforgiveable. While that hatred at State is institutional, I at no time figured anyone would act against any American personnel. I have a hard time believing that would be the case. But I cannot say it could not have happened. You should know that they did seem to be most interested in whether STAR was considering using any foreign nationals to effect a resolution. While I gave them generalities about case status, information that they could have gotten from the Tribunal Administrator in the Hague, I specifically told them that I had no knowledge about any foreign national consultants or advisors. You should also know that Mark O has contacted my office and complained about what was happening with Tunesia and whether it might be happening with the Iranian case. I refused to discuss the matter with him but none of us should trust him. I would not be surprised to learn that he was in direct contact with officials in the State Department. What Mark O does not realize is that he is not as well regarded at Foggy Bottom as he thinks he is. If he persists in making a nuisance of himself with me, or I learn anything from the State Department about attempts to interject himself in this case, you will be the first that I call." Jack said, "I cannot ask for more. Thank you, Roger. Maybe you are not as big an SOB as I thought. Have a great day, Roger." After the call Jack thought a bit. Certainly moving ahead rapidly to conclude a deal with Iran was not going to make the State Department happy. Would they be willing to take out those who are leading STAR in that direction? It was something to think about. How did Mark O figure in all of this? What is his game?

He thought about all the information that Roger had shared a bit and picked up the phone and called Askari who answered on the first ring. "Jack, peace be with you", he said. "Askari, according to Roger, the State Department is most interested if STAR has hired any Iranian advisors or consultants. Make sure that you are properly registered so that if we get to that point, everything is on the up and up. In any event, your possible involvement will be under scrutiny so take that into account. Also, if I was a target, be aware that someone is not playing by the rules. So watch your back. Jack paused before ending the call, and said, "may peace be with you."

CHAPTER 18 — THE BREAK

Jack and Kate needed a break. She had worked herself near to death making sure that Jack had been doing his rehabilitation exercises, kept up with the proper nutritional plan, got their twin daughters off to high school and school sports activities, and she made sure they were doing well in their precollege classes. She was completely immersed in planning their campus visits to colleges later in the year. She was keeping the family focused while Jack had jumped back into work. She had contacted the local bike store and found an inexpensive bike trainer that could be set up using an old bike that Jack had put up on a rack in the garage and removing the rear wheel. Coupled with the trainer, it would allow Jack, Kate, or the girls to safely mount and ride silently in the basement. No fear of traffic, wet or cold weather, and Kate could make sure that Jack did not overdo it in the recovery ahead. But now his leg had healed enough to get back in the water and that was what this trip was all about. Bermuda was the destination. It had been the site of two important events in their lives. First their quicky honeymoon during Jack's first year at Villanova Law. It had been only two days over the brief Columbus Day weekend. The honeymoon had been a tossup between a few hour drive to the Poconos or an hour or an hour flight from the Philadelphia airport to Hamilton, Bermuda. The second was a visit Jack made nearly a decade later when he had returned to finalize one of the most important corporate transactions in STAR history. The purchase of a Philadelphia refining company which had been acquired by a Swede along with numerous marketing and pipeline operations along the East coast of the US. The Swede and his family were living in Bermuda and wanted to finalize the corporate acquisition by STAR. The Swede felt that it might be possible to improve his tax position by concluding the agreements in Bermuda. Jack had always been dubious about the tax angle. Jack and his team, in collaboration with the attorneys for the Swede, worked round the clock to finalize the deal. When the deal was to be signed, the STAR team decided to have their spouses join them in Hamilton for the ensuing celebration. Kate, when she heard about the invitation, dropped everything, found an agreeable neighbor to watch the twins and jumped on the first available flight to Bermuda. That trip and the time they spent together was just as memorable as their honeymoon. This break, as short as it would be, would prove to be as important to them as either of their first two visits.

The hotel sat overlooking the Atlantic Ocean and a beautiful golf course. It was exactly as they remembered it years ago. Jack and Kate checked in and immediately changed their clothes before walking down to the beach. Jack's first swim in weeks was magnificent. Kate joined him a few yards into the water and playfully dunked him under the incoming waves. Jack in turned grabbed Kate around the waist and pulled her under. The water was refreshing and as clear as they had remembered it. There they were as playful as kids again, knowing that they were as young as they ever would be. That night, after a long afternoon in their room, they sat in the main dining room, next to the enormous glass windows overlooking the ocean lit then by the rising moon. It was everything they had hoped it would be. Jack was free of the office distractions that always seemed to intrude into their marriage. It was a glorious three days. At the airport waiting for the plane to board, Jack checked his voicemail messages using the payphone near the boarding gate. He found three messages from Ella that Askari had called and needed to see him in DC next week when Askari got back from abroad. Jack boarded and the thoughts of the Iranian project filled his mind on the flight back to Philadelphia. Kate watched him during the trip and could tell when he changed from vacation mode to work mode. The change was obvious. He had that Look.

CHAPTER 19— INSIGHTS

Jack dozed on the Metroliner to DC drifting in and out of memories of Bermuda and what he might hear from Askari this morning. Looking back over the past few months, he realized that this project had consumed him completely. It was exhilarating but he also needed to find time for the routine parts of his legal practice. He loved answering calls from clients in the field, directing them to his staff for resolution, solving a crisis with a well-reasoned answer. The corporate cost analysists would never understand completely the value a corporate counselor contributed each day. Well, a task for another day, Jack thought. At Askari's suggestion they agreed to meet at the patio outside the Caffe. Classes were now in session and they were alone.

Jack spoke first after their warm greeting. "How was the trip." Askari said that it went well and he had a few observations he gathered from his sources. "Jack, the Iranian legal team thinks that Roger is an obstacle to resolving this matter unless STAR and Pacific want to go to the mat and let the tribunal decide the case. Jack, it is my feeling that the Iranian government and the IOC will fight to the end not to pay anything if the tribunal awards even a small amount. Iran and its institutions have to get over their long held belief that Americans hate Iran and its people. That will take a great deal of effort. But they are a proud people and to be forced to accept a decision that in effect means that Iran was wrong from an International World View is something they just cannot accept. So my assessment is very simple. They do not fear litigation, much less a huge award because they have no intention of paying. Even understanding that the funds in the NY banks are not entirely under their control because of the freeze on funds in the US, they would do anything in their power to obstruct or delay the inevitable outcome.

They are very good at that as you know. The problems that caused this dispute arose a decade ago but in their view, it is as if it just happened." Jack said nothing but nodded waiting for Askari to complete his report.

Askari resumed his observations, "They see Roger, for what he is, a tool, an advocate but more than that, they feel he cannot be trusted to give the companies the truth. But they feel the same about their outside attorneys which is not entirely a surprise. While there have been meetings between the lawyers over the last decade, the subject of those sessions have focused on the mechanics of the case and not the differences between the parties. They have no illusions that any resolution other than a favorable decision will have any impact on how the world thinks of Iran or its IOC. They think that it will take a long time to change that and this case will not affect that one way or another. Certainly, that is the Iranian governmental point of view. But within IOC, there are voices that point out the reality. The oil is there. It will be produced. It needs to be sold. That time is near. The potential buyers, when it is that time, will need to be reassured that IOC is a reliable producer and seller of crude and that the crude they sell is free of claims or liens. In short Iran will need to reenter the market with a commodity they can freely sell. It is not enough to sell to outcast countries. The ability to sell to the West is important. This case and the disputes around Iranian crude are a big hurdle to overcome. Jack, that is your strength and their possible weakness. Not the claim per se. Not an adverse judgement of the tribunal. It is the possibility of reemerging as a reliable source of crude with the claims behind them."

Jack did not miss a beat. "Askari that is very powerful. That is complete confirmation of what I am believe STAR should do. Take a step, an important step in that process. Do you feel that if I inject myself as the representative of STAR at the table, I will be received the same way Roger is? Have we been so tainted by the image that Roger has presented that it cannot be overcome; that it will be a barrier so high it cannot be hurdled? I think that you are both an insightful guy and are able to judge people fairly and honestly. Tell me, truthfully, how you think I would be perceived."

"Jack, I have great faith in your honesty and sincerity. You are direct and, in my view, would come across just as I see you. But with many eyes looking across the table at you, it is probable that they will all look at you as if looking at a diamond, a stone with so many facets. It will take their entire team to assess the truth of what you say. It will take the truth and a direct no nonsense presentation of a proposal to come to a good conclusion. I think that the time may be right for a meeting and a suggested path to resolve the matter." Jack said, "I agree. I will think about doing just that. But if you have any suggestions, I would appreciate it if you would share them with me. Oh, by the way, have you made any headway with the scrolls?" Askari said, "I will tell you they look like lists of names, dates and dollar amounts arranged chronologically. The dollar amounts are quite large. The names are in some code I did not decipher. It might be money that exchanged hands or money owed. At any rate, it dates to the period 1973 to 1979. I cannot determine what the payments are for or what might have been received in exchange for the payments. But I fear that were we to decipher the names and understand what the funds are for it may not be as helpful to your negotiations as you first thought. I am so sorry I cannot tell you more. Of course, the fact of this document's existence may be more important than what it says. I would hold onto the originals if I were you. They might be useful at the right time. But there may be people on one side or another of this controversy that may not want this to be revealed. Maybe, God forbid, it is both sides."

CHAPTER 20— THE PIVOT

Jack contacted Roger's office that afternoon and asked to meet with him in the Dulles offices. When he got there Jack asked if he could conference in Tom from his offices in LA. Jack knew Tom would be available as Jack had called and updated Tom immediately after his conversation with Askari. He had offered to Tom the opportunity to talk with Askari before the meeting with Roger but Tom declined. Once everyone was ready, Jack began, "I would like you to suggest to your counterpart that it might be a good idea for the two sides to get together in the next month or so in London or Paris or another mutually agreeable location. At this point I would not feel that the Hague would be the best site of such a meeting as it might appear we were using the location of the tribunal as a threat. Of course, if they want to meet there, I have no objection. The meeting should be under the terms of a written agreement barring either side from using the statements of the other party in proceedings before the tribunal. That would be signed before we discuss anything in such a meeting. The purpose of the meeting should be rather vague but we should be prepared to discuss the recent changes to the process for release of frozen funds should events occur where using the protocols were necessary. We would also like to introduce the Company's team that is responsible for handling this case. Certainly, it is appropriate in light of the spinoff of EPOC, now Neptune, and the transfers of authority to a new team at STAR. We would cover the authorities in Pacific as well. Let them know we understand that there have been internal changes within IOC and the role of the government's relationship with IOC. A meeting involving the decision makers might be helpful as the parties move forward in the case. If the atmosphere is right, perhaps it might lend itself to a deeper discussion of each party's objectives relative to the case. I would like you to point out that, while the

Dulles firm would be attending such a meeting, particularly for the discussions of the finer points of the new US process for the release of funds, outside counsel would not be involved in much of the discussions between the parties. We would expect the same approach from the Iranian side. Lawyers would be available, but it would be the position of STAR and Pacific, not to have the lawyers in the way of frank and open discussions." Jack said, "we should have in our hip pocket a broad settlement proposal but it would only be put on the table by mutual agreement between STAR and Pacific." Roger asked, "What possible reason beyond a discussion of the payment protocol would justify a meeting. Why would Iran come to such a meeting?" Jack said, "Our intelligence sources indicate that Iran assumes it will have to litigate this matter to the bitter end and that if that is the outcome they will do everything to delay payment into the next Century. On the other hand, I am led to believe that internally they are of the view if a negotiated settlement were possible, one that they had a hand in fashioning, it might help their image and future commercial opportunities in the near term. I want to begin to test that concept and the best way I see to do that is to begin. "You cannot have a closing without an opening, as one of my early mentors used to say. In the meantime, STAR will internally determine what its settlement benchmarks should be. Hopefully Pacific will do the same. I do not intend to share them with the other side or with anyone outside either company until it is appropriate. And I mean 'anyone'." Roger responded, "I understand your approach. I feel that you are projecting a position of weakness that may jeopardize the case down the line. But if they are agreeable to a meeting, we can manage it and see where we are at the time." They wrapped up the call and Roger promised to report back on the possible meeting dates and location when he heard from the Iranian lawyers.

Jack phoned Askari to brief him. Again Askari, out of concerns of others hearing what they had to say, agreed to meet Jack outside the Caffe. When they got together Jack said, "we are putting into motion a "Beginning" by requesting a meeting in which principals from each side would attend. Outside lawyers will be excused at the right time and the principals will be encouraged to openly discuss their positions. Nothing discussed will be permitted to be used in the litigation. We would expect all parties to sign an agreement to that effect before the meeting begins. I want to convey that our side is willing to discuss ways to resolve this matter if Iran is. I want both sides to 'hear' what is important to the other side. But both must listen and 'hear,' 'really hear' what the other side is saying and feel free to share what is important to them. If you could, please convey to your sources that we want to 'listen' and learn and share. Hopefully, that will be the message they hear from Roger but using a back channel, through you, maybe we can put his message in the right context." Askari nodded his head approvingly and said he would proceed "cautiously."

CHAPTER 21 — THE OPENING

The meeting was set in London on September 1, Jack and his team planned to arrive the day before. Even though he would arrive in better condition flying business class or first class, Jack and his team elected to travel economy. It would have clearly been within Company policy to fly first class given the length of the flight but Jack chose not to spend the money. He felt that he could not complain about how much the case was costing and spend the money on a first class plane ticket. As he boarded the plane that evening, he noted that Roger and several of his partners were sharing a glass of white wine in first class. Jack nodded as he walked by Roger's seat back to the rear of the plane to where he and his team would sit.

Dreams are a complicated thing. Authors claim that they have benefited from or even be inspired by their dreams. Certainly, musicians have been known to awake in the middle of a dream with a pencil in hand jotting down in a notebook, words or notes to a hit tune. A few people Jack knew would tell him that they could even control their dreams. They claimed they could decide in advance what they planned to dream about. But when questioned, the dream deciders had to admit that they simply could not predict how the initial thought would play out in their dream world. They could start at a beginning point but somewhere in the middle, the story would go off the rails. Even more is the case for trying not to dream of a subject or to come back another night and try to change an ending. Just not going to happen. But themes can repeat again and again; sometimes you just have no control over them. And so it was, during the flight to London.

Jack, for those few hours after a rubber chicken dinner and a glass of wine and before the early dawn over Ireland, leaned back in his seat and fell into a deep sleep. His mind reconstructed the day he had left the Tanker Yabucoa and went ashore in Iran and traveled to the exploration site. This dream was in technicolor. It came with stereo. He was there, just as he remembered. His mind had replayed many intricate details, but the dialog was lacking any meaningful words. He saw the crowds of protestors; he saw the documents and disks being placed in his backpack; and then, he seemed to sense, as he was leaving the exploration site, someone had come up to him. Someone had touched his back as he was leaving. He saw a face he had not seen at the time. His dream continued. He was suddenly in the waters off Kharg Island, paddling for his life and he was being left behind. The Tanker was leaving him. He was struggling. He would not reach it. He felt the warm water engulf him. He was drowning. The backpack was going to take him to the bottom. He would die. He heard a boat coming to him and as it reached him, he heard and felt a bang as he was jolted out of his sleep. At first, he did not know where he was. Suddenly he was back in the present. The plane had landed at Heathrow. The flight was in London. During the approach, the flight attendant has made sure that he was his seat belt was properly fastened and his seat was properly fixed, all without waking him. Once the plane landed and he got his overnight bags and briefcase, and looked around the other passengers exiting, his team looked at him closely. The feelings he had about the meeting and the determination he had, they had as well. They did not know all the other thoughts that were swirling about in his mind.

CHAPTER 22 — THE MEETING

Ella had set the arrangements in motion for the meeting at the renowned Lanesborough Hotel near Hyde Park and Buckingham Palace. Rooms had been blocked out for all participants to reserve themselves. A large meeting room for the general discussions, together with two separate breakout rooms were reserved but it was up to the two parties to decide whether to avail themselves of the breakout rooms. Ella had arranged to have the main meeting room well stocked with refreshments throughout the day, including lunch if required. Each party had confirmed in advance the number of attendees. Jack had instructed Ella to communicate to the hotel that there were to be no alcoholic beverages available or stocked in any refreshment stands or bars in any of the meeting rooms. He had seen how routine it was for businesses with corporate offices in London to routinely serve all kinds of liquor with lunch and afternoon refreshments. Jack never bought into that practice himself. Each side was expected to split the costs of the meeting and Jack felt there was no need to start out on the wrong foot with the Iranian delegation by serving alcoholic beverages or expecting them to pay a share of the cost of same. Although the meeting was not to begin before 10 am, Jack was buzzing around the lobby dealing with catering services and checking out the readiness of the meeting room and eliminating all signage that referred to the type of meeting to take place or who the parties were. He made sure the meeting room was in his name, Jack Stone, omitting any reference to either of the American Companies or the Iranian Oil Company. It was well known in the oil industry that the press and competitors got great intelligence from the central billboards in key hotels frequented by the players in the industry. All careful preparations of secrecy and confidentiality could be blown when the meeting rooms and the names of the real participants were posted in the lobby. Thank goodness for Ella.

Jack had been alerted from the Dulles firm regarding the possible attendees from the Iranian side. It should include: Seyyed Ahmadi, director of Legal Services and an advisor to the President of Iran; Rezaei Mohseni, Vice President of IOC, Ali Jafari, Lawyer for IOC, Amir Rostami, legal attaché and advisor in the Iranian Office of Legal affairs and Arash Hosseini, Chief Counsel in the Iranian Office of Legal Affairs and an advisor to Ali Khamenei who had been in de facto control of Iran since 1989. Jack had reviewed the list with Askari and learned that Arash Hosseini was probably going to be the chief protagonist and spokesman for the Iranian side not only because of his experience but his closeness to Khamenei. Roger had confirmed that he would be the strongest voice for a litigated solution and most likely to advocate a meaningless settlement offer and the most likely to view any settlement proposal by STAR as a belief that we viewed out litigation position as fatally flawed and weak. Jack had told Roger that he was thankful for his views. At this stage of the discussions, Jack had felt that it was inadvisable to bring Askari into the meetings. As he was thinking through his decision on this strategy, he remembered settlement discussions he had had a few years before with a company from Greece. There the Greeks during settlement discussions conferred among themselves in Greek, often loud enough for Jack's side to hear but not understand because of a lack of proficiency in Greek language. That time he had brought a classmate from law school Baldo Papadopoulos into the meetings as counsel. Baldo was a proficient international negotiator. After a brief introduction of Baldo, the discussions were held completely in English, including any sidebar discussions among the Greek team. At the end of the day a favorable resolution was reached. After the settlement was a done deal, Jack revealed to the Greek delegation that Baldo neither spoke or understood Greek. But he had a Greek name of course. The Greeks, believing Baldo would understand every sidebar discussion they conducted in Greek, had felt ambushed by bringing Baldo to the discussions. Baldo's presence was a factor. Both delegations broke out in laughter when they realized the ruse. Baldo and Jack never forgot that deal. Askari would be useful down the road if they got that far. He understood the language and the Iranians would know that.

The plans were for Mike Shepard and Tom to attend for Pacific and Jack and Joe Camp for STAR. Roger and Abood both would attend. When all were seated and had their refreshments of choice, each side introduced themselves and shared their role with the respective company or organization. It seemed clear to Jack from the introductions that Hoesseni would control any discussion from the other side. Jack was intrigued by the way in which both sides sat during the discussions. The Iranians sat at one end of the table instead of across from the oil company delegation. Jack thought this odd. It was as if they were staying close to the exit to facilitate a quick departure.

Jack began to speak once the introductions were through. His opening remarks shocked all in the room. He said, "this is the first time we have brought both sides together since the death of your spiritual leader, the Aytollah Khomeini and I want to express my personal condolences at the loss of his life and extend to you and your new spiritual leader, Aytollah Khamenei peace and blessings." He bowed slightly to Hoesseni and to the members of the Iranian team. While shocked by the American's sincere words, they all bowed slightly in return. While Roger and his team of lawyers looked apoplectic at Jack, Jack felt that the entire mood of the meeting had been altered. Jack continued, and noted that although he was responsible for the litigation between the parties, he was a business lawyer that was charged with the responsibility of achieving the proper outcome for the business itself. He said, "the parties to this dispute should look forward to the day when normal business relations would resume. In that environment, proper business relationships will suffer disputes which must be resolved on a commercial basis. Maybe these meetings can serve as an example for others now and in the future that disputes can be resolved if the parties so desire. In that regard we would like to show you the calculation of the value of the assets that IOC and Iran have taken from us." Jack asked Abood to turn his computer on and link it up to a projector and show a case. Jack went on to describe the graph now lit up on the screen and how it shows first the amount of oil that both STAR and Pacific believe would be recovered without the taking by Iran. The next graph, Jack pointed out, shows the amount of production year by year not only from the first 5 wells but also the remaining wells that probably would be drilled over the next ten years of the lease. Finally, the next graph Abood put up, Jack indicated shows the low, middle and high oil price projections for the entire period of projected production. Jack then stated; "some of you, I know, have seen similar slides as these because earlier versions have been entered into evidence for the upcoming hearings of the arbitration panel next year. These have been updated slightly to reflect revised oil price projections. My goal here is not to convince you to resolve this matter based upon our demands but to consider this: the leases have real value to us and the royalties that would have been paid to Iran and IOC are substantial. Iran and IOC have lost those royalties because we were prevented from completing our work on the lease. The Iranian government has lost these funds and so have the Iranian people. The dilemma that Iran has faced since this dispute arose is clear, absent a resolution by a verdict of the arbitration panel or by settlement, sales from this lease are subject to claims by these two companies until they have been fully compensated. That is an impenetrable cloud of uncertainty. It is in the interest of both parties to cut a path through this cloud if we can." It was at this time that Roger and his entire legal team as one arose, grabbed their papers and quietly left the meeting room without explanation. Was it planned in advance? Or was this a reaction to his speech.

At the finish of Jack's remarks, Hosseini stood and, looking quickly at the rest of the Iranian delegation, leaned a bit forward and said, "Thank you Mr. Stone for your heartfelt words, may blessings be upon you. You have given us much to think about." He sat down and Iranian team leaned into one another and began a discussion intended only for their side to comprehend. They were certain that no one on Jack's side of the table would understand a word that was being spoken. And they were right. Seeing that the Iranian discussions might take a while, Jack suggested that the parties break their discussions for a half hour and then resume. He suggested that the Iranians were free to stay in their place and the American delegation would retire to their predesignated meeting room down the hall. At that Jack and the entire oil company delegation got up and left the room to the Iranians. Jack added, as they were leaving, "if you need more time, feel free to send a representative to our meeting room and we will return when you are ready to resume discussions."

The half hour came and went. Roger was gone and had not left a message. Abood reported that he had gotten a call from one of his former partners and that Roger was so upset with the position that Jack had put forth, he just went to the airport and intended to leave on the next flight back to DC. Jack walked back to the large meeting room and found it empty except for Ali Jafari, a young attorney with the Iranian team. Feeling that Ali was there for a purpose, Jack asked him what was going on. Ali responded, "I have been instructed to tell you that there would be no negotiations to settle the case at this time. We appreciate you setting up this meeting and in particular your opening remarks about our late spiritual leader but, with respect to the amount of your claim, if you are trying to scare us with its size, you should know it will not work. But we listened to your words after the slide show carefully. We will not make a move to settle this matter. We cannot. I have been told by our spokesman, that if you want to settle this, you need to find a way to do it. We cannot do it for you. That is what I have been instructed to say." Jack listened and responded in this way: "I thank you for the message you were asked to give me. I am not sure that I understand the meaning of it but will give it much thought. But this is what I believe. If you did not want to engage in a meeting to discuss the possibility of resolution short of litigation, you would not have come to London. You would have stayed home in Teheran. That message, I would have understood plainly. I appreciate that you came many thousands of miles and did meet. Please tell Mr. Hosseini that I thank him for his honesty and if we have future meetings, I would like him to select the location and the date. You have my contact information." Jack then began to turn away, thinking how he was going to tell his team that they were done for the day when Ali stopped him. "Mr. Stone, you may not remember me, but we have met before." Jack stared at his face and thought of his dream on the flight to London and the events that the dream called to mind. I know this man he thought. Ali continued, "I was one of the young students that surrounded the fence of your exploration offices ten years ago. I resumed my studies and am a lawyer today. Our revolution allowed me to do that. It also gave me deep feelings about this oil field. It is our heritage. This fight is not who the Iranian people are. We want to look beyond this but for now we cannot. We look to you to find a way. I remember that day. I had been instructed by one of the student leaders to give you something. I did and then you were gone. You look the same, maybe a little older." He stopped and then said: "May peace and blessings be on you." He turned and left the room.

Jack went to the breakout room and briefed his team and basically left them with the thought, let us give this some time and figure out whether there is a back channel way to light a fire under them. Mike then said," Joe and I feel this was a good start. We think we are in good hands. Keep us posted and when you need us, we will be with you at the table. Hopefully, just to sign a deal." Then they left for the airport. Jack went upstairs to his room and was surprised that his clothes were neatly folded and placed on the bed and that his wife was smiling and sitting at the desk in the bedroom and waiting for his return. Kate had flown in that morning and checked in his room and was planning to stay for several days touring the gardens around the city while he was negotiating his deal. She knew he would be so emersed in his potential deal that she felt she needed to steal some time between meetings to keep the romance alive. Jack was overjoyed to see her and his kiss told her that. All the exhaustion and frustration from the meetings downstairs went out of his mind and body. He told her he was so glad she had come and that he would have a few days to tour the City with her if she wanted company. She said dinner was several hours away and that that they should use the time slowly and …

Jack got up early the next morning and looked over at the phone and realized that the message light was on. He had not noticed it as he and Kate were busy. He picked up the phone and heard a recording from an unidentified person. He did not recognize the voice, but it clearly was an American. The message said: "You are off the reservation Mr. Stone. If you continue, the mishap that occurred in Pennsylvania will be the least of your concerns." The time of the recording indicated that the message had been left after this meeting downstairs with the Iranians had adjourned.

Jack called his office and left messages for Ella that he was going to alter his return trip to Philadelphia by two days and be back in the office the third day. That would give him two days to see the City of London with Kate. They saw the sights on a whirl wind tour of the City, hitting Westminster, St Paul's Cathedral, the changing of the guard at Buckingham Palace, the Tower of London and even Wimbledon. It was a glorious break in the schedule. Of course, Jack had taken the time to call back to the headquarters and report to Jason who seemed pleased that a deal was not in the immediate horizon. Jack did not think too much about that. Both evenings Jack and his wife spent the time relaxing at dinner, reviewing the highlights of the day of touring and examining the postcards they had collected. It was difficult deciding which cards to send back to the States to family and friends and which to treat as keepsakes. Before he dozed off both of those nights, he reviewed the day of tours and thought about several occasions each day when he swore that he was being watched. Each time he had looked around he saw nothing out of sorts, but the feeling remained. He thought that I must be losing it or my mind is playing tricks on me or possibly they were awfully good. I will have to look quicker and more closely. Was it really our own government officials watching or was it someone else? Before they left, Kate said she wanted to share something with Jack.

CHAPTER 23 — THE LOOK

Kate looked at Jack and said, "Jack, when you first came into the room from you meeting the other day, you had that look on your face but when you saw me, it instantly went away. That look, you know it. I know it. This time together has been good for you and for us. I am glad that the look is gone, because that look is really scary. It is you, but it is not. Whenever I have seen it, I wonder if you are there behind the face or where you really are. I know I don't want to be in the way. You look like you could run through walls. That look tells me something: you have a objective and are determined to achieve it; but you know you only can if you go all out. You can't control what you do to get there." Jack knew the first time that Kate had seen him like that. It was a race. Oh, Kate had seen him race over the years, even in high school. But usually she was not near the finish of his races then. This was some years later. After he had been working at STAR for several years, he had taken up competitive running again. The STAR running team was looking for an older runner that would fill out the roster for a competitive team race along the Wissahickon trail near Chestnut Hill, Pennsylvania. It would be a race with many great individual runners, both men and women. In addition, there was a corporate team event matching several corporate running teams against one another. There was a City Corporate Cup trophy at stake, and the STAR team was determined to win the Cup. Each six person team had to have at least one female and one person over 40 . The old guy slot was added to avoid a team being composed of a bunch of recent college graduates. Terry and Steve had been part of the team. Jack was all in and he trained intensely for the competition. His family had seen him race when he was fully invested in an important race while growing up. One of his brothers, Joe, said to him, "Jack, when you are racing, you are, at times, no different than an addict. You need the feel of adrenaline running through your body that this racing business gives you. It's as if you need a fix and that nothing will get in your way to get it." Jack had just laughed at Joe's assertion, but it did make him think about why he needed to run and compete. He liked it and maybe it was what made him who he was.

The big race along the Wissahickon Creek in Fairmont Park in Philadelphia, Pennsylvania was scheduled for late Fall. It was to be held on a trail that had been cut through the Park and was known as the Forbidden Trail. It was a multiuse path that was used by walkers, trail runners, walkers, dirt and trailbikes, horses and even horse carriages, though usually for special events. The trail was frequently covered in piles of horse litter. In the Fall it was covered in leaves that fell from the canopy of trees that made running on the trail seem like a run through a long dark tunnel, interspersed with openings to the sky of brilliant sunshine. It was a glorious place to run. The trail itself was covered in a rough grit which is sometimes referred to as a cinder surface. The tracks at public schools back in the days before artificial surfaces used this type of material as it was easy to maintain and never seemed to wear out. When it did, the cost of resurfacing or repairing it was "dirt cheap." The Forbidden Trail was cool in the Summer and sheltered in the winter months, the trail wound down to the Schuylkill River from Chestnut Hill following the Wissahickon Creek. But a Fall run was just spectacular with the autumn leaves painting a background that Van Gogh would have been proud to have called his own. The race, a 3.1 mile event, would start at the trail entrance, run downhill along the trail about a mile and a half and then immediately turn back uphill to the finish where the race had begun.

Now there are all types of racers. Most just run their race. Some just run like hell and then walk the remaining mile until their legs cool down. The more experienced know whether they have the stamina to run full out for the distance, maybe leaving a little extra for the end. Some understand pacing better and start out a bit slower and finish strong with a ferocious kick. Yet others will pick out a person who they think they can beat and just pace off their shoulder and outkick them at the finish, happy to make the competition do all the work of pacing. Others may actually be better than most of the others in the race but choose to play with other runners, much like a cat likes to play with its prey before consuming it. Jack would run into one like that in this race. Of course, a race with a severe downhill followed by a good uphill would offer its own challenges, even to good runners.

Jack knew what pace he could run in order to finish well in support of his STAR team. The gun sounded and Jack and a field of about 50 set off from the start. He had noticed a runner that must have been from another corporate team dressed in red. This was not Jack's favorite color for a running shirt during the Summer. But a Fall run made it seem OK. Jack liked to give folks he was competing against nicknames. This one had a short beard and instantly was deemed "Red Beard", even though his beard was not red. Jack kept his pace and saw a good downhill ahead and took advantage of the slope and passed several runners, including Red Beard who looked at Jack as he passed him. Soon it seemed he and Red Beard were locked in a personal race even though Jack was sticking to his planned race strategy. He had planned it out. He would keep himself under control, out in about a 6 minute per mile pace and back slightly under 6 minutes, per mile, even though it was all uphill, most of the way back. At times Red Beard seemed to be attached to Jack's shoulder and at others Red Beard would surge ahead and cut immediately in front of Jack, seemingly in a deliberate attempt to cause Jack to break his stride and back off his pace. And it would not be unusual for Red Beard to take advantage of Jack's downshift in pace to accelerate and attempt to place a few extra yards between them. Competition is a great thing. It gets the juices going but this was not really that. It was bordering on a total lack of sportsmanship. Red Beard had done this a few times. He had also taken advantage of curves in the trail where the path had narrowed a bit. Then Red Beard had jostled Jack, using his elbow to obtain an advantage. Jack made a decision. If there was any way that Jack could beat this guy fairly, Jack would do everything he could to do so. This was more than a race. But it still was about pace. Maybe then the "look" took control.

They had made the turn and Jack, with about 1.5 miles to go, was still on his pace but perhaps about 20 feet behind Red Beard. Jack loved hills and this one was going to be a challenge if he wanted to hold his pace. The downhill had really helped him for the first half of the race. It would take an effort on the way back, but racing Red Beard would make the hills almost invisible. Jack set out and gradually picked up the pace, zeroing on Red Beard's back and soon he was on top of him and closing. He avoided sprinting as he knew it would cost him in the end of the race; so slow and steady was his style as he closed the next few feet. Red Beard saw him out of the corner of his eye and Jack slowly pulled by and kept on going. As they approached a curve in the trail, Jack glanced back and saw he had about a 10-yard lead, but he knew better. Red Beard, coming out of the bend in the trail put on a tremendous sprint and opened up a 5 yard lead, still using his technique of cutting right in front of Jack as he passed. There was now about a mile to the finish, uphill mostly, but leveling off at the finish line. Again, Jack slowly pushed forward and soon the 5-yard lead Red Beard had was gone. Stride by stride they continued, yard by yard and the finish line was dead ahead, but Jack knew his trail. The last hill made the finish line nearly invisible and so it would be easy to misjudge the effort needed to carry the race to the finish line. At the top, maybe Red Beard would be vulnerable, particularly if he thought he had crushed Jack on that last hill and so they continued to run side by side. Then as they hit the last hill, Red Beard surged full out to the top, thinking he had put Jack away. Jack had just tucked in behind Red Beard and kept the same pace. At the top of the hill the finish was just ahead and Jack now abreast of Red Beard stayed steady as Jack glanced to his right. He could see that Red Beard was angry beyond belief. He thought he had put away this old guy. But that old guy was keeping pace. Then Red Beard pulled out all stops and made one last burst to the finish. Jack waited and waited, keeping just slightly behind his opponent, and then gritting his teeth, his eyes wide open and determined not to lose he surged one last time and dove through the air and crashed beyond the finish line clipping Red Beard at the tape. It was an out of body experience for Jack. For Red Beard, it was a crushing defeat.

Kate had seen the whole thing, the effort, the dive, the look on Jack's face, the win and the slide and the crash. His whole body was covered in cinders which mostly stuck to his running shirt but his hands, arms and knees were another story. The cinders just tore up his skin, leaving him a bloody mess. Years later, the cinders were still visible on his knees and in the palm of his hands. Picking himself off the ground, Jack slowly got up and walked over to Red Beard and offered his hand. Red Beard just refused it. Jack was surprised as Red Beard just walked away from him. Jack thought a bit as the other finishers crossed the line. He looked around and found Red Beard in a crowd of his corporate teammates. Jack again walked up to Red Beard, offered his hand, and said he wanted to thank him for the race. This time he got a response from Red Beard but still a refusal to shake hands. Red Beard said: "If you wanted the race that bad to dive over the finish line, you can have it" and walked away. Jack thought, a handshake with a person having that little class was not ever worth it. Jack never forgot that race, the determination he showed and the dive at the finish line and Red Beard's behavior. Kate did not either. The look on Jack's face as he surged ahead and caught Red Beard at the finish line scared her. She did not want to see it again very soon. But she had as he had entered the room after the meeting. Jack told her that all was good. He knew what he needed to do to bring this case to a good closure. He would finish this thing. There was nothing else he could do but finish it.

CHAPTER 24 — OFFERING THE BONE

Jack got back in the office the following Monday and sat with his team and listened to their take on the meeting in London. Steve made it clear to Jack that the entire team felt Roger should just be gone. They just did not see any reason to go over the events that led to his departure. Jack asked the team to focus on the way forward. There were two views that emerged from the team. One that Iran would never budge off the litigation track; they just would not make the first move. The second was that if the only way to resolve this within the year was through negotiation, STAR and Pacific would have to make the first move and that would signal, if Roger was right, that we were weak and that the end result would be a lowball outcome. Jack felt that these were both reasonable observations. After everyone had their say, Jack said, "what if neither side perceives that they are making an offer. In the context of a mediation, which this is not, a mediator typically meets with the parties separately. Then the mediator tells one party what they think the other's position might be and draws out a reaction. Then in sequence, the mediator draws the parties closer without either side making a firm proposal directly until the mediator senses the parties are so close that they conclude a deal. So, in that sense no proposal is actually made by either party. No one feels they are being weak. No one is locked into positions as the discussions are without prejudice. Maybe we can find a mediator or see if we can create an atmosphere in the way we interact that mimics a mediation. We would of course need an experienced negotiator or mediator to make that happen. Another approach might be to have an emissary go to the Iranians and throw up possible outcomes that would convince the other side to come back to the table with a framework of a deal set out. Let me discuss this with Askari and see what he thinks about either of these approaches." Steve and the team looked at Jack and nodded in unison.

After the meeting he drafted a Fax to Roger . It read:

"I appreciate all the work you and your firm have performed for the past eight or nine years on behalf of the Company. The Company has decided to move in another direction with this litigation. Please transfer all existing files to the Abood firm, bring you billings up to date and submit invoices for unbilled time. The Company values your commitment to it throughout the past and trusts that this transition will be done as smoothly and seamlessly as possible. If down the road, I feel there is a need for your counsel, I trust that we may count on your future availability. If following this disengagement, you receive inquiries or communication from the Iranians or the IOC, please direct them to me."

He sent it to the team and asked them to finalize it and send it out under his name when they were satisfied. Before he left the conference room, Steve said: "I suggest that you might as well add that "any inquiries from the US government also be directed to you. He is bound to talk with them anyway, so you may as well make it clear that you know that will be the case." Jack nodded and said "add it along with any other minor changes which are necessary." He went to his office. There he asked Ella to arrange a meeting with Askari. She found out he was planning to come to Penn for a seminar the next day and arranged a meeting between Jack and he the following afternoon at 30th Steet Station.

Jack walked from his offices to the meeting site and found a room off one of the cavernous halls that Ella had secured for a private meeting. The station was one of the depression era structures that is an architectural marvel with dominating statues and ceilings that could hold a punt from an NFL kicker. Askari loved to walk and the Penn campus was close by the station. He arrived refreshed and they timed their arrivals almost to the minute. Jack and Askari greeted each other warmly. This was becoming more than a business relationship. There was real trust. Jack thought if this mediation thing can be done, this is the man to do it. Let's see how this conversation plays out he thought. Jack updated him on the meeting in London and his disappointment that nothing meaningful had been accomplished. He observed that Askari had never indicated that a deal could be done or even that the meeting would be productive; only that the meeting would happen and who would be there. He broached a possible role that Askari could perform if he was willing. First the role of a mediator. Could he serve as a neutral mediator between the parties or find a mediator willing to do so and whether that could work. Askari considered this and remarked: "well I could hardly serve as a neutral mediator given our initial meetings and engagement." Jack immediately responded, "Askari, it was inappropriate for me to have suggested that course. Please forgive me for suggesting it. I am brainstorming and looking for a solution. Is there a way to create an atmosphere in which the Iranian side could sense the atmosphere of a mediation without an actual mediator being involved. We could exclude litigation counsel and deal principal to principal but with each party having a pretty good idea what the parameters of a deal would be. Could we make that happen. Would it work? Could you use your backdoor connections to lay the groundwork for that to happen." As Jack laid out his thinking out loud, Askari was reading Jack and his body language and began to nod. He was silent for a few moments and then in a measured way responded: "Here is what I see. I see that you are a very sincere man, a trustworthy man who says what he means. I am so glad that they heard your remarks about the passing of the Aytollah Khomeini. That was important and I am certain it will help in the end. I believe that the Iranians can be convinced to send someone to a meeting who has the ultimate authority to conclude a deal but they must be assured that a resolution is highly possible and that the representatives of the company are sincere in reaching a deal. I believe they already see you as sincere and I will make sure they feel you are trustworthy as well. I will assure them that you say what you mean and that you mean what you say. My most recent trip identified who the decision maker would be. As you have gone over the attendees with me, it is clear that the key figure did not attend and that in part was your biggest problem. No authority was given to the Iranian team. It seems they were just there to gather intelligence. While I cannot be a mediator, I can continue to be a trustworthy emissary to the right people. If you trust me to have your financial objectives, I can test to see if they are achievable under the right circumstances. They will not, in my opinion just accept what you expect to achieve. They will want to test that boundary much like a hungry dog will take many passes at your offer of a bone before he comes close enough to you to take it. He will be warry of you at first; he will believe you will trick him; he will believe, just like that proverbial dog, you might possibly strike him or even take the bone away completely. Your goal is to not flinch, not become incensed if he does not respond as you think he should. You cannot become frustrated when he backs off. Nor can you cease to be steady. My goal is to tell them you are real and that the parameters of a deal are real; that the bone is real and it is good; that you are to be trusted and can be believed. This will create the right atmosphere for a deal: having the right participants there; identify the right person to be the spokesman and have both parties feel the deal is probable. This I can do for you if you trust me to do it. I do not say that I can make a deal happen but I can help you move closer than you are. If you want me to try, I will do everything within my power to make sure that if Iran is willing to meet again, the right decision maker will be present and that they will understand that your proposed outcome is in the ballpark and is real. If you think that is worthwhile, I will do it. It will take time and a trip abroad, but I believe it can be done, God willing." Jack said "lets plan this out then. Let's make this happen. And by the way, make sure that they select the meeting site. I will bring the original copies of the scrolls if that adds anything to influence the momentum."

CHAPTER 25 — THE HAGUE

The first of November was here. The time had changed back to Standard Time and Askari had returned from his trip abroad with news. Just as important to Jack was his own recovery from his "accident." He was completely cleared to put 100% weight on his damaged leg and the swimming he had done as well as the limited cycling he had been doing each morning on the stationary bike was helping his mind heal as well. That coming weekend would mark the running of the NY City Marathon and the first Florida Ironman race in Panama City, Florida. There were things that were pleasant distractions to think about as he contacted Askari by phone at his office. The message he had received that morning on his desk was that Askari had good news to report. Askari said in his conversation: "we should meet soon and discretely in DC. Oh, and Jack, take precautions. It is more important that ever!" That shocked Jack because he had come to believe he had been overly paranoid and that all these feelings he had felt after the last meeting were an overreaction. But now? What did Askari mean? Well, we will see, Jack thought.

They found a private room on the GW Law School campus and sat quietly for a moment, both collecting their thoughts. Askari said that he had taken two separate trips to meet with his contacts. He did not say who and he did not disclose where these meetings had taken place, except to say they had taken place outside of Iran. Before he got into detail with his report, he asked," Jack have you ever seen Teheran?" When Jack shook his head and replied that he had only been to Iran briefly the one time when the students surrounded the exploration offices of STAR. Askari continued, "I spent a few years with my parents there. It was a most beautiful place. If conditions between the US and Iran ever get better, you should go for yourself.

Of course, it assuredly is not the same as it was when I was a child. Maybe that day will come." Askari continued, "First there are forces dead set against any deal. On the one hand the US State Department is dead set against almost anything you want to do except taking scalps through an arbitration verdict. I have heard this from many of my colleagues at GW that work as consultants to the State Department. But of course, your Lobbyists in your Washington, DC office must know of this." Jack nodded. Askari continued, "In your own industry, there are at least 3 major oil companies each of whom have similar claims to yours and I am hearing they do not want to see a smaller group such as you and your partner company creating a precedent for future resolutions. As they are way behind your efforts from a timing point of view, they fear that if you are first, they will be severely damaged in their efforts to seek a huge resolution. Moreover, the frozen funds are not unlimited so there is always a fear that little will be left if the first companies settle early. That I must leave with you to deal with, but obviously collaborating with your competitors has antitrust implications if you are not careful." He paused to let all this sink in. And then he continued: "From my end I want to report that there are at least 3 or four factions in Iran that have different views of this possible negotiation. And I say possible but that may be too negative a characterization. In any event there are those who want a return to the days of the Shah, along with the improvement of relationships with the world. They never mention the Shah in talking about their movement but it is clear to me, based on who their families are, what they are all about. Another group wants a more democratic country and have appealed to Khaminei pointing out he and his predecessor had championed this when they were both in exile in France. Yet another group is pushing alignment with the Soviets both political and economical. And then there is the inner group surrounding Khamenei, that seek to protect his position in navigating the objectives of all these groups and more. They are a dangerous group, willing to impose their ideas of a country ruled under the rules of Islam, up to and including a suppression of the opposition, even to the point of assassination and more. But there are pragmatists among them. I have met with some of them and they believe a resolution of all the Oil Company litigation is in the best short and long term interests of Iran. I have suggested that, rather than try to settle all at one time, take your two companies' case and use it as the model for the industry. Then the floodgates will be open. I spent time talking with some key players and they are willing to meet and to test your sincerity, your grit. They will shortly contact you and suggest a meeting in the Hague where the arbitration panel does hold its sessions and will send a chief negotiator that has the authority to bind Iran. But I believe he will test you and your partner company. His name is Amir Rostami. He is a sincere man but very much in Khamenei's camp. They have suggested that I come to the Hague and help with the discussions if that is your wish. But I wish to point out that he and I have had confrontations going back to our childhood days and it could be a problem. I have been assured it would not get in the way but I wanted to alert you to the possibility. I have shared with my contacts in Iran that your framework would involve a deal in which the unpaid cargo was forgiven and that there would be a payment of funds from the frozen account in an amount both parties find acceptable. They have suggested that any undelivered drilling supplies would be transferred to Iran, with no requirement that it be delivered to Iran. So it would be their problem to deal with sanctions in the future." Askari asked Jack what he thought. Jack's first instinct was to say it was a "home run" and then thought in soccer terms as that analogy was better suited to Askari's background, said it was a "goal."

Then Jack turned back to the discussions about the opposition. "How dangerous are the various groups that are dead set against a possible deal? Could any of them be involved in 'accidents' or engage in surveillance or disruptions and if so, who were the most likely players in that." Askari responded, "All I can tell you is that the Iranian factions do have the ability to reach out to the West and cause great harm but I have no information that any of that has happened or will happen. But anything is possible", said Askari. He continued, "I have stronger feelings about the ripples that Mark O has made within the State Department and his connections within the Oil Industry. That is the most likely connection between 'accidents' and 'opposition'. When you hear from Iran, and I believe you will be the one to receive the communication, let me know and I will make time to attend the session.

It was only a day or so later that Jack received the call from the Iranian's outside counsel extending an invitation to meet with a delegation from Iran and the IOC on November 15 at the Hotel des Indes in the Hague. Jack responded that his delegation from the two companies would attend. The Hotel is a 5-Star, destination that is located in the heart of the Hague, a short walk from the US Embassy and the tribunal offices of the International Court of Justice hearing the dispute between the two oil companies and Iran. This session would not be attended at the beginning of the session by the business executives given how Iranian delegation had behaved. The executives had agreed to hang back in Scotland, play a little golf and be available when needed. In the interim they would delegate to Jack and Tom, the authority to make any and all proposals that were consistent with the broad objectives of the companies. Jack contacted both Askari and Abood and asked them to come and be prepared to negotiate a final deal at the meeting if conditions were right. He called Jason and informed him of the meeting and then listened to Jason respond. What he heard shocked him to the core. Jason said, "I need to relate a few things that have come up. First, nothing I tell you changes the charge you have to bring this case to a conclusion but I want to make you aware of some information that has come to my attention. Two Major oil companies are asking whether we would change the timing of any negotiations with Iran if not end the negotiations completely. They fear we are jeopardizing their financial position. Jack, I feel certain you will return with a great deal and that if those that come to the table after you get more which I don't believe will happen, that is 'tough crap', and if they don't get as much as they think they are entitled to get, that is their own fault not yours. The second piece of news, is that Mark O has been spending time among those in the anti-Iran click at the State Department. It seems his goal and those of this click is to do anything in their power to disrupt Iran's path to a return to a respectable member of the western world. They view you as a disrupter of their strategy. Of course, this is our government we are talking about and I believe that our government will support an American company trying to do what the law allows. I do not know what this click is all about but in retrospect, I cannot completely rule out that they were behind your 'accident'. So, watch yourself." Jack finally responded after a brief pause to digest the news, "I plan to go and get the best deal I can and will let the chips fall where they may. I will watch out for myself." As he hung up, he closed his eyes and had a vision of two black SUVs or Vans speeding off as he and Dave lay on the highway. Were those black SUVs or Vans Government vehicles? He could not be certain.

By the 14th of November, Jack and his team were assembled in the Hague. An office had been set up by Abood with his computers and word processers plugged in and ready to go. By then the effects of jet lag were worn away, and Jack after inspecting Abood's office had decided to take a walk. About two blocks from the hotel was a BMW showroom and Jack, long an admirer of fancy new European cars, spotted a shiny new BMW in the showroom. He was taken aback by what he saw. It was a black convertible, a car he had never seen before. But this one was more unique than he could have imagined. This one had doors that rolled down into the chassis of the car with the click of a key fob. Walking into the showroom to see for himself how this marvelous vehicle worked, the salesman, wearing a suit that probably cost 5 times more than the suit Jack had worn that morning, asked him whether he was an American. Jack said,"Yes I am." The salesman said he could arrange to have it shipped directly to the states without export or import duties if he was with the US Embassy. Jack chuckled and said "I don't work at the Embassy. By the way how much does a car like this cost?" When he heard the number and computed the exchange rate, Jack knew that a car like that would not be affordable in his lifetime. He trudged back to the Hotel and checked out the planned meeting room and breakout rooms as well as assured himself that the hotel management would not identify the actual names of the parties in the Hotel Bulletin Board. The designated meeting room was spectacular. It had a 12-foot ceiling and a long table made of mahogany with comfortable adjustable seats. He also double checked with the manager to be assured that no alcoholic beverages would be available in any of the rooms. The Manager on duty said that his hotel was the host hotel for many middle eastern companies and that they knew the drill. He also reminded Jack that many Dutch citizens were Muslim and that the Hotel knew what they were doing. Jack nodded and walked away.

The next morning, Jack got up and went for a slow deliberate run, his first in several months. The Hotel was not too far from the waters of the North Sea. He felt the morning breeze hit his face as he ran alone along the beach homes and restaurants along the beach. He was just beginning to fall into the zone, that place where nothing is going on in the consciousness except the wind and the air and the sky began to turn colors in the morning sun, when out of the side of his eye, he felt or heard or saw the car, a black one, maybe a Van. He had been running against traffic, so the car had come from his right rear and was traveling fast and had swiftly moved from his right towards his left. A voice cried out "move!" Fortunately, his reflexes were good and he quickly stepped left between two parked cars and slammed into one as the black car missed him. Unfortunately, the car he hit was also struck by the attacking car. He could see no one around that could have shouted out "move."

He could see that the attacking car had deeply black tinted windows but he could not see the driver as it glanced off the parked car and sped off down the road. He checked his body parts to make sure that he was not seriously injured and then knocked on the door of the home behind the car that had been hit. He informed the man answering the door that his car had been hit and damaged by a car that had left the scene of the accident. He could not give him any information beyond that it was black and had damage on its left side. His 'running high' irrevocably lost, Jack returned on the sidewalks to the Hotel des Indes. He did some thinking on his way back. An accident? He not only thought-NO! This time he knew -NOT! NOT A CHANCE THIS WAS AN ACCIDENT! But how would he explain this to the local police? They would just not understand, much less discover, who the culprit really was. He would just have to watch his back even more.

Before the meeting started, Tom came up to Jack and said, "I received a message from the US Embassy that they want to have us brief them after our meeting this morning." Jack nodded and said, 'OK if you think we should." The time had arrived and both delegations were seated, introductions were made. Jack acknowledged them, including Ali. All the players for the Iranian team were the same except Amir Rostami. Unlike the first meeting, Amir and his team positioned themselves at the middle of the table opposite Jack and Tom. The two companies team included Abood, Bert Williams, Steve Barron, Terry Land and Askari. When Askari introduced himself, there was a murmuring from the Iranian side. He was known. His presence disturbed their normal sidebar discussions in Iranian and would keep them from passing notes in Farsei. It was clear that they knew he had connections back home in Teheran and that unsettled them. But they said nothing. His introduction was in English and he made it clear that his role was not to interject himself in the conversations as he turned the floor over to Jack. Jack thanked Amir and his team for inviting them to the Hague and indicated that this meeting he hoped would bring the two sides closer together, perhaps even to an agreeable outcome but if not at least to an understanding of each sides' position. Amir extended his thanks for Jack's team for accepting the invitation and for coming. After a pause, Amir began to explain that after a time to reflect on the first meeting and to study the companies remarks during that meeting their side felt that the first meeting had not ended the way in which the Iranians wished it had. Although he did point out that Jack's heartfelt expression to the Iranians of the recent loss of their spiritual leader was noted. He then added, "let us begin again."

So Jack laid out the formula for a basic settlement: "first, we would receive a just and fair payment for the leases from the frozen funds that are now held in the US Banks in New York under US control. Jack added that all claims against the companies, including claims for the shipments of crude that each company had lifted but not paid for would be forgiven. In addition the companies would transfer title to all drilling pipe and equipment that was currently stored in England at the Holms warehouse, upon payment by Iran of the storage charges since the date of the seizure of the oil fields; and third, the oil companies would release any and all claims regarding the exploration agreements and leases; and finally there would be mutual releases by all parties to the tribunal proceedings. Amir asked for a few moments to confer with his team and suggested a break, indicating that a representative would come to their breakout room when they were ready to respond.

After about a half an hour, Ali knocked on the companies' meeting room and said this team was ready to resume the session. When they arrived in the meeting room, Amir and his team were already seated and ready to proceed. Once everyone was ready, Amir nodded to Jack and also to Askari and spoke: "We have understood the outline of the structure of a deal that you have described. We find that the points you have outlined are acceptable to us with the proviso that a final agreement presenting the basic terms of a deal must be prepared in both English and Farsi and executed by all parties. That would leave us with the unanswered question from our point of view being, how much is to be paid out of the frozen funds, if any. What is a just and fair payment. If what I have proposed is acceptable, how shall we proceed toward that amount." Jack responded immediately, "of course the final agreement shall be in both English and Farsi. The English version will prevail. How would you like to proceed to reach a just and fair amount. One consideration you should factor in your deliberation is that we, as publicly owned companies will be required to report to our regulators and our shareholders any material settlement. I say that because, in the case of my company, the terms of a settlement as to the crude purchase would be 'material'. That means it will have to be reported in our filings with the SEC and a public announcement of the settlement would have to be made. I want to make sure that you are aware of that. Our deal if we reach on cannot be a secret deal. Is that going to be a problem?" Amir leaned over to Ali and whispered and Ali nodded. Amir then asked Ali something further and again Ali nodded. Amir then spoke, "yes, we understand that the substantial points of any deal we make are not going to be secret but will have to be disclosed to all our constituencies, shareholders, regulators and our government officials. Both sides have obligations that make secrecy unattainable. Openness is good and it will be observed in any deal, regardless of who may think otherwise." Jack then asked again what he had asked earlier, "how shall we proceed?" "Maybe a review of the factors that drive your claim might be a good start," said Amir.

So they spent the afternoon having Abood show slides that took a claim with an assumption of zero successful wells drilled to 25 and then the volume of the assumed reservoirs found to the barrels of oil that could be recovered and the numbers of barrels that could be produced and at what rate per year and finally an assumption on the future price of crude. That generates any number of cases depending on the weight of any particular assumption. The resulting calculations then generate a high, medium and low case under any assumption. Jack pointed out that for purposes of the discussions now, "we can ignore the cases that assume additional leases would be awarded in the future to the Companies based on the success on developing the initial leases." Jack indicated that Iran was not bound to grant future leases to the Companies and could and probably should retain the freedom to contract with anyone for future leases. He said "The oil is an Iranian 'treasure' and Iran should be expected to do as it seemed fit with that 'treasure' in the future. But even ignoring that future upside, the size of the high case could be argued before a tribunal as unrealistically high." But Jack also observed "it was unrealistic to argue successfully before the tribunal that that zero recoveries from the leases was going to be the ruling by the tribunal. Iran must have determined that the leases should be "taken" from the Companies because they had real economic value to Iran. If they really thought the leases had zero value, one would have thought Iran would have invited STAR and Pacific back to finish the drilling just to prove the leases had no value. You did not ask. I think you must have felt that the oil beneath the leases was of value to your country. We would argue we would have come back if asked. So that is where we are, battling about the future value of leases not drilled to completion. Regardless of whether your decision was based on moral or political reasons, the decision has real dollar consequences. And we can translate that, as we have with these graphs to real dollars and the values of those dollars over time. This was what the parties should be considering."

Jack stopped at that point before determining what to say next and then began again. "To that end, I think we can each disregard a case that gives us every dollar of the high case and that you should know that we cannot agree on a zero case either. Jack paused and let Amir absorb the fact that Jack had taken the high case off the table, and said, "let's look at the several medium cases and see if each side can look at the assumptions again and find some basis to justify a middle ground to justify a settlement. It is not necessary that we agree on any one or two assumptions but it is a framework to work within." After another pause, Askari spoke out for the first time, "another way to look at this is for each party to share directly or indirectly, without prejudice, what they would not accept, Iran as a high number and the Companies as a low number and then see if there is a gap. I am willing to receive the numbers in confidence and only report to the two parties if there is reason to continue today with discussions, or you can share directly with each other if that is preferred. The parties said mutually that it was a good time to break for lunch.

Tom reminded Jack of their sit down at the US Embassy. So, they took a short walk to the Embassy building. They were expected. L. Jackson Vandross greeted them, failed to indicate his position or provide a business card and spent a moment or two just glaring at Jack. Jack began to share in broad terms what had transpired in the meeting that morning. Vandross would not hear of it and said, "I know exactly what transpired this morning. Don't you realize that our national security may be threatened by a quick settlement of your case? And who is this person Askari. Who is he working for? Is he related to the late Lt General Amahad Husseini? What credentials do you have that suggest you are qualified to be negotiating directly with the Government of Iran and its principal national oil company." Jack was quick to respond: "look Mr. Vandross, it is clear to me and Tom that you have caused the meeting rooms of the participants in our settlement conference to be bugged. Bugging American citizens and American Company officials is outrageous, if not illegal. It is clear that there is no need for us to come here and brief you if you know everything that is going on. I agreed to meet and as far as I am concerned, I have done what I agreed to do. This meeting is over. We believe we are acting in the best interest of our American Companies by seeking the most in settlement dollars and terms that we can achieve. You should be doing everything possible to help us by not throwing obstacles in our paths. And I am sure you already know this, I was the victim of a second attempt to take me out by vehicle while on my morning run today. I am not in a mood to play nice and dumb. I am neither." Jack and Tom left the Embassy, slowly walking back to the Des Indes and casually looking over their shoulders for a tail. As they walked, Jack said: "I hope you noticed that Mr. Vandross did not seem surprised by my near accident this morning nor deny that his office had anything to do with it or that all of the rooms were bugged!" Tom said, "It is clear we were bugged and probably the Iranian side as well. I am no longer sure which side our government is on."

They got back to the breakout room where lunch was set up for their team. Jack and Tom pulled Askari aside and Jack said quietly, "we are sure that the meeting room is bugged and I want you to pass that message on to the Iranians. In reality, I think everything we say, we might have an obligation to share with our government. But I am honor bound to negotiate this deal fairly. I need no 'sign stealing' done on our behalf that would give us an unfair advantage in our discussions. Everything is to be conducted above board and with professionalism. We both feel that way. Tell Amir that." Askari left the breakout room and sought out Amir. About a half an hour later, Askari returned and reported back on his discussions. He said: "Amir said 'we suspected as much' and he was impressed with your words which I conveyed to him. He shared with me a range of numbers showing where they would like to be at the end of the negotiations. He asked me to convey them to you. He also shared with me in confidence the number beyond which they could not and would not go. While I will honor his request, I will share with you that the two parties are close to having their brackets intersect. This exercise has been worthwhile." Jack and Tom both nodded and took Askari into the breakout room and reconvened the team to discuss next move. The range of suggestions covered the map. On the one hand presenting an enormous number might be counterproductive. Showing a modest reduction might be viewed the same, a nonstarter. Yet a deep move might be viewed as a weak opening bid. The consensus was to provide Askari with a one-time drop-dead number that exceeded Iran's walk away number but was fair and supportable based upon the Abood numbers. Jack instructed Askari to point out that that it would be withdrawn if a quick deal could not be agreed to in principle that afternoon. All members of the oil company team agreed. Askari left the room. Tom and Jack conferred and agreed that both Joe Camp and Mike should be informed that we may be close and might consider altering their golf outing in Aberdeen and come to the Hague for a signing the day after tomorrow. They could return to the States on the morning flight from Schiphol that morning. Both Jack and Tom were adamant that they wanted a firm written agreement signed by all parties rather than a one-page non-binding agreement in principle. Such letters of intent or term sheets might have to be disclosed and they could be rejected once the public is notified. Competitors have been known in large transactions to swoop down and try to top the bid disclosed prematurely. In terms of a settlement that was unlikely to happen but with the State Department lingering in the weeds, anything was possible. Better to drive to the final contract and pound the stakes into the ground. Well, this may all be wishful thinking, thought Jack. Jack thought he better call Jason now and give him a heads up, which he did. Jason was always hard for Jack to read. Now over the phone it was impossible.

Jack took a walk to the BMW show room and got the attention of the salesman. He guessed that 'salesman' was not the highbrow title that the representative had used earlier. Maybe it was Director of Sales and Exports. What was his name? Hans Richter? Yes, that was his name and title. He shook Hans' hand and pressed close to him and whispered, "Hans, I hope you have concluded your deals with the State Department employees because they may not be in town much longer." He turned and walked out of the showroom, looking back at the most gorgeous car he had ever seen. He could just imagine Kate driving it with the top down through the thoroughfares of the Main Line of Philadelphia. She would have loved it. Too bad!

CHAPTER 26 — FINISH THE DEAL

Askari returned and suggested that they grab a buffet dinner from the main dining room and return to the main meeting room at 8 PM for a final session with the Iranians. Sounded good to Jack. Askari said little to Jack over the quick meal but his demeanor was upbeat and the team seemed to read that as had Jack. Jack had been surprised to find a station serving large pancakes with fruit and thick honey and other syrups as an entrée. They were amazing. Jack had four; Tom had five.

Sharply at 8 PM the parties gathered, greeted one another and Amir began the session. "We understand the proposal that Mr. Askari brought to us and if it is agreeable to you, it is to Iran and IOC." Tom and Jack quickly looked at each other. They had accepted their number! This thing would be over. They controlled their emotions in silence. Amir continued, "The number plus the terms you outlined this morning should be incorporated in a written agreement and documented tonight. We would be prepared to sign both the agreement in English and in Farsi when they are in final form. Can your signatories be here in a day after we have agreed on all language." Jack said they would be here. Then the work began. By morning the English version of the agreement was in final form and shared with the Iranians who in turn shared it with their litigation counsel. As Abood was there already, the review of the English version was less complicated. The Farsi version was next and Askari reviewed the final version and agreed it was correct. Abood had previously disclosed that he only understood the Iranian language at a rudimentary level. All notifications had been made to the tribunal and all necessary pass codes and approvals obtained. Both Joe Camp and Mike were scheduled to arrive later that afternoon. The signing was set for 9 am the following morning. Things were being set into motion with the funds to be released from the NY banks holding the frozen funds. All had been marshalled with City Bank and in lieu of a wire, two accounts, one in Pacific's name and the other in STAR would be transferred to the respective companies upon receipt of an executed release of funds signed by Iran and IOC. All was set to roll as of the opening of business in NY the following morning. So there was a built-in window of about 5 hours between signing and the transfer of funds. Nothing could happen right? The lawyers on all sides began to release the adrenalin and come down from their emotional highs. Askari found out he could catch a flight that evening, shook hands all around and departed. Everyone was in a good mood until…

Ali showed up at 6:30 the next morning in the main dining room and said he wanted to talk over a cup of coffee. He had a copy of the Farsi version of the agreement in his hand. All the original documents were printed on high end paper and the ink on each page was duly raised from the paper. They had been set on the table overnight ready for signing set for 9 am. He said he had reviewed the papers one last time late last night. The English version was approved for execution. But he had discovered that the lawyers had made one small mistake on one of the pages in translating from English to Farsi. The English word was represented by a character, different from the correct symbol. He had instructed his staff to make the change and substitute the page and reprint the Farsi version of the documents for signing. The English version was correct in all respects. It was the original Farsi translation that was incorrect. Ali pointed out the mistake to Amir and Amir had agreed with Ali to correct it and rerun the Farsi version for signature. Ali was now in an awkward position, clearly if he had just brought one page to the signing with the change and made the change in front of the lawyers for the other side, it might have raised no serious questions. But what was being presented was a really sticky wicket. Rather than a single page, he was presenting an entire document with the single page with the corrected symbol substituted. Looking at the Farsi document, one could not tell whether it was the same as the initial translation with a single change or an entirely new document. So each page had to be verified and then if it was only a single character on one page, Jack had to "believe" Ali that the new character was the proper one to choose to make the substitution. Askari had flown out the night before and was with his wife somewhere that he could not be reached by phone; that Jack had realized was a strategic error on his part. The bigger fuss that Jack's side made of the issue, the greater insult to Amir's honor. It might even suggest that the American companies were waffling on the whole deal over what the Iranian's viewed as a typo. Abood was a deer in the headlights. Suddenly Vandross from the State Department showed up at the door of the signing room with someone that claimed to be an expert in Farsi. Vandross suggested to Tom that the expert read the entire document to assure that what Amir was saying was correct. Jack showed Vandross the door and asked him to leave at once but directed this expert to double check the document. This Abood, Tom and Jack had already started to do themselves. They were nearly finished when the so called "expert" was half way finished his review. Then he too was finished. Indeed a review line by line symbol by symbol by Tom, Jack and this expert concluded that the only change was as Ali had represented, the next to the last page of the Farsi version 8 lines from the bottom. Jack asked the so called "expert" to tell everyone what the difference was between the two symbols, the one in the formal document on the table and the document proposed by the Iranians to be used as the signing document. The expert looked at Jack blankly and muttered that he had no idea. In fact, this State Department official could neither read nor write or speak Farsi. Jack thought "what a fiasco." He threw the guy out of the room, adding a push as he was leaving. During this document review, Amir had entered into the room and observed what could only be viewed as the blind leading the blind and he seemed so upset, it was doubtful he would sign even if the American Companies accepted the Farsi version as presented. Tom was nervous. Jack looked at Abood who whispered, "I do not know enough Farsi to opine on this. It is a matter of trust or you can wait a day or so. Maybe you should talk with Ali before you decide. Remember, the English version controls so the risk is very small." At that point Jack walked over to Ali and calmly looked him in the eye and asked him to tell him what the change in symbol meant. It was, Ali said, a different way of expressing the concept of 'full' in context of a full release that was consistent with the correct Farsi usage. Ali did indicate that the original symbol that had been used in the first translation was not wrong. But this substituted symbol was the preferred usage. Now, Ali pointed out this was no longer about the symbol. It was now a point of trust, of honor, of integrity of the Iranians that was being challenged. Ali reported that it was now being discussed among the Iranian team that the American Companies seemed to be returning to the attitude that their lawyers had exhibited for the last 10 years. Ali said that Amir felt he was being called a liar over an inconsequential word that did not change the substance of the deal. And as Ali pointed out, the Companies lawyers had made it clear in both documents that in the event of a difference between the English version and the Farsi version, the English version would prevail. Jack's big words of trust and openness were now being challenged. Jack thanked him for his candor and turned to Joe and Mike and said, "I know that Joe and you Mike are going to have to leave now if you are to make your flights. But Joe, we should sign this deal as presented. The change they made is not material and I feel that the risk is so small to be nonexistent. I would ask you to delegate to me your authority to sign on behalf of STAR if and when I am satisfied with the Farsi document and allow Tom and Mike to resolve the issue of the symbol after we sign. Whether the Iranian's are willing to sign if both companies do not both sign at the same time, I cannot say. They have not indicated to me they would. But I believe we should show our continued good faith and commitment to this deal. If there is indeed a conflict between the two documents the English version will govern. The documents are clear on this. Joe, are we good?" Joe said, "if you are ok, I am good. I delegate to you authority to sign on behalf of STAR if you are satisfied." Joe then turned to Mike, who added, "Tom, I delegate the authority I have to you to sign the settlement agreement with the changes proposed by Amir when you are satisfied." At that Joe and Mike got up and left.

Now the eyes in the room were on Jack. Jack asked Ali if he would be agreeable to using the original Farsi signature documents with the substitution of the single page that contained the correction Ali had made and have that document signed by all Jack said, "I am prepared on behalf of STAR to sign that final version with the corrected page." He added, "of course I will only sign if that is agreeable to everybody." Tom nodded first, then Ali and Amir and then everyone else agreed. The tension in the room was suddenly gone. While Ali was in the copy room, Jack and Amir reviewed the bank payment instructions that would be sent jointly at 9 am NY Time, about 3 PM in the Hague. The bank was expecting the call and accompanying numbers. Ali returned with the copies and placed them in each packet. The documents were ready and Jack signed his versions in English and in Farsi on behalf of STAR and Tom added his signature to both on behalf of Pacific. Bert Williams witnessed both signatures. Amir signed the documents and Ali witnessed his signature. A ten-year saga came to an honorable conclusion. The money transferred as agreed. The deal was done. It represented the largest litigation settlement in the history of STAR to date but in an environment of "what have you done for me lately" that fact was soon forgotten in Jack's career. Jack had long been aware that the expression "you are only as good as your last memo" was as good as carved into the entrance to the Legal department at the STAR offices.

Jack returned to Philadelphia with little fanfare, although Jason did come to his office and shake his hand, but he said absolutely nothing about the accomplishment in the Hague. Jack would bury himself in unattended legal matters and resume training for some long distance race that always seemed out there for Jack to do. He found a race that suited him. Ironman Coeur d'Alene in Idaho seemed ideal. It would be his first full triathlon and he trained like a phenom. What made this race unique was that the lake water was fed by the melting snow from the mountains and the height of the bike climbs was ferocious. The run was hilly but nowhere as difficult as the hills of Pennsylvania.

He quickly got over his ego being crushed by non-recognition of his Hague accomplishment and the miles of cycling and running and the laps in the local pool took him to another place, far away from Iran, London, the Hague and the intrigue of the State Department. Kate had made sure that he was fueled and rested and comforted as he ramped up his training. He knew just as he knew in the Hague, he would finish even if it took all he had. And he had. He swam 2.4 miles in the sub 50 degree waters that had fed off the melting snow caps of the mountains, pedaled 112 miles in the blazing hills of the foothills of those same mountains, fixing two flat tires on the course and struggling for 26.2 miles, much in the evening and then in darkness, hearing only the occasional shuffling of running shoes some running, others walking near him. Then he saw Kate jumping up and down at the finish, screaming his name. She nearly knocked him down as she hugged and kissed him, celebrating his accomplishment. That was worth more than any business or professional accolade he had ever received at STAR. Each triathlon he did after that was as much of an accomplishment as his first but there can only be one "first."

CHAPTER 27— FINISH THE RACE

Jack returned from the journey through his mind and found himself still at the edge of the Choptank looking at the tent and its surrounding cast of characters, now after more than an hour into the afternoon. Normally, the day before a big race, he spent the time hydrating and wolfing down carbohydrates. There was still time to get into the water and stretch out and get a leisurely swim before a 2 mile ride and a mile run fast enough to get the heart rate up. Having left the memories behind, that is what he did. The waters of the Choptank were at the perfect temperature, the brown water, ugly looking, to those desiring the clear waters of the Caribbean but clean and a little brackish because of the mixture of the waters from the Choptank river and the salt from the Chesapeake. He felt soothed as he mounted his tri bike and rode a mile or so through downtown Cambridge, acknowledging the waves of locals excited to see one of the triathletes that had come to town. Then a short pick me up run, consisting of a slow jog interspersed with 10 yard sprints which moved the heart rate up, stretched out the legs and helped with the visual preparation for the sprint to the finish line the next night.

Jack came back to the edge of the Choptank and checked on his gear before he headed back to the hotel. Awaiting Jack at the water's edge was Ali. They greeted one another like long standing friends. They found an old picnic table and sat. After Jack brought Ali up to date on his retirement from STAR and his accomplishments in running and triathlons and writing. Ali, taking all that in, said he wanted to bring Jack up to date on what he had gone through over the past 20 years. He looked away as he started to tell his story, "The principal negotiator, Amir, fell out of favor quickly after the deal was announced and he went into hiding. He avoided capture for 10 years, although members of his family were jailed and suffered greatly. By the time he was captured, another faction had achieved enough influence that he was released and no longer subject to prosecution. Due to ineptness or maybe because the oil was not ever there, the expropriated fields never yielded any oil. I myself fled the country around the time Amir was being hunted, fearing I was on some hit list. I used my legal training to land a position as an advisor to the government of an Arab country that you may not have ever heard of and have traveled extensively with the members of its royal family, serving as a translator and consultant on Western matters. I have become a fitness fanatic and have been working with the emir's family, particularly the swimming discipline. That is why you saw me swimming with him during the practice swim this morning. I am a citizen of that country now and I have not been back to Iran for the past 20 years." Then he asked about Askari. Jack said, "Askari passed away about 5 years ago. It was a peaceful death and some of his ashes had been returned to Tehran where they were spread in the neighborhood he had been living as a child. He had said to me many times that he longed for the beauty of Tehran as he had remembered as a child. His family sent me a video of the spreading of his ashes and watching it, I wept. Tom went on the General Counsel of Pacific. STAR never acknowledged what I had done. I am glad you stopped by and that you remembered me. You took me back to a time when I had something to complete and we did. Ali, we all did it together. I do have a question for you though." Ali asked his what it was. Jack said, "were you there in the Haag when I nearly was hit by a car, yelling for me to 'move.' Was that you?" Ali nodded his head. "I was out that morning for a walk and saw the car coming and just yelled. Never could tell who it was though. Just instinct, yelling out." Jack said, "Thank you for that Ali. One last thing, I know you know I still have the capsules you gave me so many years ago. I finally deciphered them. I believe it shows a series of payments between Iranian officials and American politicians and officials but I cannot be sure. For now I intend to keep them. It has kept me safe I believe. If anything happens to me, don't be surprised if you get them back to use as you see fit."

THE END